The Nearness of God

THE NEARNESS
OF GOD

PARISH MINISTRY AS SPIRITUAL PRACTICE

Julia Gatta

Morehouse Publishing
NEW YORK · HARRISBURG · DENVER

Morehouse Publishing, 4775 Linglestown Road, Harrisburg, PA 17112
Morehouse Publishing, 445 Fifth Avenue, New York, NY 10016
Morehouse Publishing is an imprint of Church Publishing Incorporated.

Cover photo by David Skidmore, Canon for Communication for the
        Episcopal Diocese of Chicago
Cover design by Laurie Klein Westhafer
Interior design by Vicki K. Black

                Library of Congress Cataloging-in-Publication Data
Gatta, Julia, 1948–
The nearness of God : parish ministry as spiritual practice / Julia Gatta.
        p.   cm.
Includes bibliographical references.
ISBN 978-0-8192-2318-0 (pbk.)
1. Pastoral theology. 2. Pastoral theology—Episcopal Church. 3. Church work. 4. Church work—Episcopal Church. I. Title.
BV4011.3.G38 2010
253—dc22
                                                2009042009

Printed in the United States of America

10 11 12 13 14 15   10 9 8 7 6 5 4 3 2

For my friends,
Joy and Ted Coolidge

This is the life of the priest:
to dwell completely in the explicit nearness of God.

— KARL RAHNER

CONTENTS

PREFACE

*"Very truly, I tell you, the one who believes in me
will do the works that I do." (John 14:12)*

THIS BOOK REALLY began in February 1991, when I was
asked to lead a clergy retreat for the Diocese of Chicago, along
with my colleague and friend, Ted Coolidge. As we prepared our
addresses for these other clergy, most of whom were engaged in
parish ministry, we found ourselves drawn to inquire what the
ministry of Jesus *in us* is like, more from the inside than from the
outside. We tried to reflect on how we were being formed in
Christ as we engage in characteristic priestly ministries—preaching, eucharistic celebration, or the ministry of healing, for example. Since then, I have attempted to develop and refine this way
of thinking about parish ministry in clergy retreats in other dioceses and settings. I wish to register my gratitude to the many
priests and deacons who encouraged me to expand and eventually
publish those addresses, which form the core of this book.

I have also drawn on several other sources: the wise counsel of
my own mentors, including those who guide us across the centuries through their writings; the clergy for whom I have been
privileged to serve as a spiritual director; my own experience as an

Episcopal priest engaged in parish ministry for twenty-five years; and more recently, my experience as a teacher of pastoral theology.

This book, then, is addressed to clergy. Another volume might deal with the theme of Christ's work in us in terms of lay ministry, although lay people could find many of the topics covered here—community, liturgy, or living within limits, for example—pertinent to their own experience in the church. They might also pick up some clues in these pages for locating signs of grace in their own lives. Still, my topic has a particular focus and is trying to address a particular need of clergy. For some time now, the pastoral vocation has seemed adrift: a calling in search of a job description. Since the middle of the twentieth century, pastoral studies have dealt almost exclusively with methods of pastoral care. Consequently, clergy have bounced from thinking of themselves as counselors to seeing themselves primarily as managers, and more recently, as leaders of their congregations and communities. In the midst of all these changes in perception and practice, a fundamental question arises: What distinguishes Christian ministry from other "helping professions"?

In response to this crisis in pastoral identity, Urban T. Holmes III, dean of the School of Theology at Sewanee until his early death in 1981, was one of the first to call the priesthood of the church back to its theological and spiritual roots. In *The Future Shape of Ministry*, one of his earliest works, Holmes challenged clergy to reclaim their vocation to mediate the transcendent mystery of God. His last book, *Spirituality for Ministry*, set forth some of the ascetical disciplines necessary for effective priestly ministry. Holmes helped priests appreciate the spiritual depth of their calling, and his influence at Sewanee, the seminary where I now teach, is still felt. Since his time, there have been encouraging signs in other quarters that pastoral theology is again taking the theological side of its vocation more seriously. We are starting to recover and articulate the Christological foundations of ministry.[1] Briefly put, Christian ministry is Christ's ministry, working through us. This book is an attempt to show what living into the ministry of

---

1. See, for example, Andrew Purves, *Reconstructing Pastoral Theology: A Christological Foundation* (Louisville: Westminster John Knox Press, 2004).

Christ might look and feel like in the sort of day-to-day situations in which clergy typically find themselves.

The New Testament does not hesitate to use the bold language of "participation" (*koinonia*) to express the transformed relationship the Christian has with God (2 Pet. 1:4). At baptism, the new Christian is immersed into Jesus' death and resurrection (Rom. 6:3–11) and is charged to "put on" Christ (Rom. 13:14; Gal. 3:27). The sacramental mystery of the eucharist continually deepens the life of Christ in the body of the church and in each believer (1 Cor. 10:16). Transformation into Christ is both the gift of God and the goal of discipleship: "I have been crucified with Christ," claims Paul, "and it is no longer I who live, but it is Christ who lives in me" (Gal. 2:19b–20).

For too long, as Andrew Purves has recently pointed out, the church has subscribed to an essentially ethical understanding of *imitatio Christi* to define the goal of Christian life and ministry. In this approach, the Jesus of the gospels becomes a time-bound moral exemplar, external to the church. It is not a large step from this sort of moralistic Christianity, whether practiced in its socially conservative or liberal forms, to an ethical theism in which the distinctively *Christian* theological content has evaporated, along with the distinctively Christian contours of discipleship and prayer. The eschatological horizon is eclipsed, and ministry becomes either a nostalgic exercise in "doing what Jesus did" or a utopian scheme to usher in the future kingdom of God on earth. By contrast, a more mystagogical understanding of both the Risen Lord and his church leads us to encounter the living Christ now through liturgy, sacraments, Scripture, and prayer. Indeed, since the ascended Lord "fills all things" (Eph. 4:10), he may be found everywhere by those who apprehend his presence by faith.

Thus Christian ministry is rooted in Christian mysticism: Christ's life in us and our life in Christ. In the Farewell Discourse in St. John's gospel, Jesus speaks and prays at length about intertwining relationships: to his Father and to the Spirit and to his disciples. He addresses their bonds with him and the disciples' connection with one another. In the charged atmosphere of the Last Supper, Jesus invites his disciples to abide in him as he al-

ready abides in them, and this sense of mutual indwelling extends
to their relation to his Father and the Spirit: "Those who love me
will keep my word, and my Father will love them, and we will
come to them and make our home with them" (John 14:23). We
are further assured that from such interpenetration our ministries
will "bear much fruit" (John 15:5). Our work does matter, although its effectiveness depends entirely on our prior relationship
to God. We are not condemned to spinning our wheels, to going
through meaningless motions. Our work is invested with a high
dignity—higher, in fact, than may feel comfortable, for Jesus in
the same passage goes on to promise that we will accomplish even
"greater works" than his own (John 14:12).

All Christian ministry, both lay and ordained, participates in
the ministry of Christ. We have all been "made to drink of the
one Spirit" who distributes various charismatic gifts in the church
(1 Cor. 12:4–13). It is that Spirit who prays in us and indeed
forms Christ in us (Rom. 8:15–17). This book seeks to identify
some of the ways the ministry of Christ might operate in those
called to serve as "pastor, priest, and teacher" in the church, as the
Ordinal of the *Book of Common Prayer* describes the work of the
presbyter.[2] I will be looking at characteristic priestly ministries to
see just how grace might show up, to notice how Christ might be
at work in us and through us. Along the way, I want to consider
some practices and habits we might cultivate to open us to this
grace and respond faithfully to it.

Because I am an Episcopal priest, I will naturally be drawing
on specifically Anglican sources, contexts, and nomenclature for
my delineation of the pastoral vocation. Yet I hope this book will
also be useful for clergy of other parts of Christ's church, from
whom I have learned much. What I will be attempting to trace are
the patterns of grace that tend to come to light as clergy are engaged in their ordinary round of duties.

I wish to thank Christopher Bryan, the editor of the *Sewanee
Theological Review,* for permission to include material from two of
my articles: "The Marriage of the Bride and the Lamb: The Cel-

---

2. *The Book of Common Prayer* (New York: Church Hymnal Corporation, 1979), 531.
All future references to the BCP are given in the text.

ebrant's Prayer in the Eucharist" (*STR* 35 [Easter 1992]) and "'If You are the Son of God, Throw Yourself Down': The Temptations of Christ in the Practice of Ministry" (*STR* 50 [Christmas 2006]). I am also grateful to John Orens, editor of *The Anglican Catholic*, for permission to incorporate material from my article "Towards Catholicity: More Than We Can Ask or Imagine" (*The Anglican Catholic* 13 [Winter 2001–2002]).

Members of St. Paul's Church in Windham, Connecticut, will recognize in these pages many aspects of the parish life I was blessed to share with them as their vicar from 1991 until 2004. I must also include my debt to the Society of St. John the Evangelist, whom I have known since my days in seminary. That community's engagement with the mysticism of the Fourth Evangelist developed, for themselves and for those associated with them, a rich field for exploring our life in God. I can remember M. Thomas Shaw, SSJE, now Bishop of Massachusetts, preaching and teaching in the 1980s about "the whole mystery of Christ" as the real context for understanding Christian life. It is a perspective that has profoundly shaped my own conception of ministry.

I am grateful to Cynthia Shattuck of Church Publishing for her early encouragement of this project and for her skillful and sensitive editing. Finally, I thank my husband, John, my dearest friend and, for nearly four decades, the first and always discerning reader of my work.

CHAPTER ONE

CALLED TOGETHER

Vocation in Community

"I believe I am so called."
(The Ordination of a Priest, BCP 531)

WITH THESE WORDS, the candidate for ordination sums up years of discernment. Our examination before the bishop seems at first to be a rather solitary moment, where we take our life in our hands and declare our own faith about our vocation: "I believe I am so called." We say it is a "call"—not a job or even a profession. Even in the case of the ordination of a bishop—where the fact of election might well be reckoned a call by God and the church—the candidate is still asked, "Are you persuaded that God has called you to the office of bishop?" (BCP 517). At no point in the ordination liturgy can we let "the process" speak for itself. Those about to be ordained, having weighed both interior and exterior evidence of God's call, must articulate the discernment that has emerged as an act of faith. Yet as we stand before the ordaining bishop, we realize that we are not alone and never will be, really. The community of faith stands all around us: the community that fostered and probed this calling, the community that tested and helped us articulate our sense of vocation, the community in which we will exercise the ministry of Christ for the rest of our lives. So even as we believe this calling ultimately comes from God, we know that the church also must confirm and speak the call to us: "Do you believe that you are truly called by God and his Church?" A vocation to holy orders is developed and examined by the church, and the grace of holy orders is conferred in the setting in which the church is most fully and charismatically the church—the Holy Eucharist.[1]

The dynamic of grace at work in all the sacraments is strikingly evident in the sacrament of orders. It involves an *epiclesis*— a prayer calling upon the Holy Spirit. Since the late Middle Ages in the West, the rite of ordination has included singing the *Veni Creator Spiritus*.[2] Charles Simeon, writing in the early nineteenth century about the ordination liturgy, pondered the significance of both the silent invocation of the Spirit just prior to the act of ordination and the singing of "a hymn which in beauty of composition and spirituality of import cannot easily be surpassed.... In this devout hymn the agency of the Holy Spirit, as the one source of light and peace and holiness is fully acknowledged, and earnestly sought as the necessary means of forming pastors after God's heart."[3]

The silence, the hymn, and the prayers of ordination all call upon the Holy Spirit. Moreover, the rite of ordination itself is situated within the eucharistic liturgy, the very place where the church finds herself on the frontiers of the age to come. The gathered liturgical community is part of the eschatological community, for the blessing of the Holy Eucharist comes to us not just from the remembered past of the Lord's Supper but also from the future promise of the Supper of the Lamb. At an ordination, we receive the *charismata* the ascended Lord showers upon the church: "The gifts he gave were that some would be apostles, some prophets, some evangelists, some pastors and teachers, to equip

---

1. This last point is made forcibly by John D. Zizioulas in his *Being as Communion: Studies in Personhood and the Church* (Crestwood, N.Y.: St. Vladimir's Seminary Press, 1985), 192–93.
2. Marion J. Hatchett, *Commentary on the American Prayer Book* (New York: The Seabury Press, 1981), 504.
3. Charles Simeon, "The Excellency of the Liturgy," in *Prayer Book Spirituality*, ed. J. Robert Wright (New York: Church Hymnal Corporation, 1989), 447.

the saints for the work of ministry, for building up the body of Christ" (Eph. 4:11–12).

We know that ordination is not conferred for our personal benefit or to satisfy our personal wishes. Without a doubt, its grace can be wonderfully redemptive for those who receive it, but it is ultimately given for the sake of others—bestowed, as St. Paul would remind us, "for the common good." Just as our initial sense of a call to orders had to be discerned within the community of faith, so we find that as we exercise that call, we are drawn more fully into the *koinonia*—the communion—of the church. We work out our salvation, we practice our ministries, within the warp and woof of church life, wherever we find ourselves.

But just where *do* we find ourselves? Typically, clergy move from cure to cure, serving several congregations over the course of their lives. In some denominations, fairly rapid turnover is required by church policy. In the Episcopal Church, the priest, with at least the tacit approval of the bishop, is usually the one who initiates a change of position. According to some statistics, the average cure these days is about seven years, which is not very long. How does the uprooting of lives that frequent relocation entails affect our rhetoric of "community," and even more seriously, our capacity to receive God's grace within particular communities?

To be sure, there are some transitions that are natural and predictable. The newly ordained curate or the more seasoned associate becomes ready to take on the broader task of rector and so leaves after a few years. Everybody expects this development to occur, and while there will be some feelings of loss, there will also be a sense of fulfillment and joy. So, too, in the case of those whose first few cures prepared them to accept wider responsibility in the church: senior pastor of a larger congregation, dean of a cathedral, seminary teacher or administrator, or bishop. And then there are those cases in which priest and parish are so ill-suited to each other in every way that their continued pastoral relationship is downright destructive. It is time to move.

But not so fast. Sometimes priest and parish need to grow into a more mature love for each other, coming to accept that the other party is not one's ideal priest or dream parish. God may have something better in mind for us than our composite portrait of the "truly committed" church. Decades ago Dietrich Bonhoeffer warned against unleashing the ruinous power of idealism gone awry. Those who approach communities of faith demanding, even inwardly, that they conform to one's "wish dream" become, in the long run, the "destroyer" of that community.[4] In recent years, some pastoral theologians have urged clergy to take to heart the witness of longer pastorates, tenures that embody God's faithfulness to us more convincingly.[5] Longer pastorates challenge the sort of theological fantasies clergy are apt to entertain about Christian community. They shape us spiritually as well as the congregations we serve by forcing us to deal, patiently and respectfully, with people whose views and desires for the church are different from our own. Longer pastorates keep us from running away from people we may find irritating or problems we cannot easily solve. Above all, they testify to the truth that Christ, rather than congruence of personality or outlook, is the foundation of the church.

The Need for Stability

The highly mobile society that characterizes the United States today holds particular challenges for the church. Few professionals live and work in the towns or cities in which they grew up. For many American adults and their children, the extended family has ceased to be part of their natural community; grandparents, aunts, uncles, and cousins are visited, at most, a few times a year. Job mobility makes and unmakes friendships. In this situation, the church can serve as a built-in community for people whose jobs have caused them to be uprooted; the desire for social connection may not be the highest motivation for joining a particular church

---

4. Dietrich Bonhoeffer, *Life Together*, trans. John W. Doberstein (San Francisco: Harper & Row: 1954), 27.
5. Eugene H. Peterson, *The Contemplative Pastor: Returning to the Art of Spiritual Direction* (Grand Rapids, Mich.: Eerdmans, 1989), 48-49; and George R. Sumner, *Being Salt: A Theology of an Ordered Church* (Eugene, Ore.: Wipf & Stock: 2007), 58.

community, but it is real. Yet the freedom we experience in mobility comes at a high emotional and social cost, and some contend that the price is too high. At any rate, should clergy simply reflect this cultural trend or challenge it by a more grounded life?

Kentucky farmer and author Wendell Berry is one of the most eloquent voices today urging commitment to a particular locale. Berry reminds us that love does not exist as a disembodied idea: "Love is never abstract. It does not adhere to the universe or the planet or the nation or the institution or the profession, but to the singular sparrows of the street, the lilies of the field, 'the least of these my brethren.'"[6] Berry's own dogged devotion to farming a parcel of land near the place where he grew up, and farming it organically, in a way that respects the discrete limitations of that tract of earth, witnesses to the means by which love becomes incarnate. Incarnation is always particular.

Lack of geographical rootedness bespeaks a more systemic problem: our restlessness and desire to have it all. The unwillingness of our affluent society to exercise prudent self-limitation has brought about an environmental crisis that is, in some respects at least, already beyond repair. We need to cultivate the Benedictine virtue of stability: the resolve to stay with this place, this parish, to burrow into its graced possibilities over the long haul. For it is only in our particular circumstances that grace is ever to be found. Reflecting on stability as a trait of character as much as an external boundary, Metropolitan Anthony Bloom has observed: "You find stability at the moment when you discover that God is everywhere, that you do not need to seek him elsewhere. . . . If you cannot find him here you will not find Him anywhere else."[7]

Stability does not imply a retreat into parochialism, shrinking the church to the scale of the local congregation; rather, it reminds us that the local community in which we find ourselves *does* matter, and matters crucially. Embracing the whole begins with a loving embrace of our actual community: the community of the natural elements of soil, landscape, and other animals; the community of our neighborhood; and the community of our faith.

---

6. Wendell Berry, *What Are People For?* (New York: North Point Press, 1990), 200.
7. Anthony Bloom, "My Monastic Life," in *Cistercian Studies* 8:2 (1973): 187–97.

True universality is found in specific communities of faith—so long as these communities remain open, at least in principle, to incorporate "all sorts and conditions" of human beings. For this reason, Greek Orthodox theologian John Zizioulas situates the local church, in the full ecclesial meaning of the term, in the diocese. By privileging geography over the human accidents of age, race, or social class, the diocese stands the best chance of being a truly catholic reality.[8]

SETTLING IN, SETTLING DOWN

My thinking about the intersection between natural communities and catholicity has been shaped by a year of living and working in Africa. For an academic term, my husband and I taught at a small, impoverished Anglican seminary in the Transkei—at that time one of the black "homelands" in the apartheid system of South Africa. At St. Bede's, we were quickly incorporated into an intense community in which everyone, students and faculty alike, lived, worked, prayed, and took meals together. We then spent a full academic year in West Africa, where my husband taught at the University of Dakar on a Fulbright Teaching Fellowship. From time to time, we would leave the city to visit remote villages in the countryside with some Peace Corps friends. Here we witnessed human community as people had lived it for millennia. It was easy to feel some romantic nostalgia for the natural society our ancestors had enjoyed but was now utterly removed from our contemporary western experience. In the closely knit family bonds and predetermined roles of those societies, it was hard to imagine anyone suffering an identity crisis much less existential angst. Life just went on, in remarkable harmony with the rhythms of nature, as it always had, full of joy and sorrow.

8. John D. Zizioulas, "The Local Church in a Perspective of Communion," in *Being as Communion: Studies in Personhood and the Church* (Crestwood, N.Y.: St. Vladimir's Seminary Press, 1985), 247–60.

Despite the evident poverty, it was hard not to feel at least a twinge of envy until eventually honesty set in: Would I really want this life, I asked myself, even if I were free to choose it? No, I would not. I realized that I treasured the freedom of the post-Enlightenment West of which I was a cultural product. I would not want to spend my working hours pounding millet with the village women, even if the price I pay for that freedom is living in a society that sometimes seems united by nothing more than our common agreement to let each of us go our separate ways.

But do we have to choose, even theoretically, between the secure but, for us, stifling community of tribal society, and the alienated individualism of the West? I think not. *We can exercise our freedom precisely by placing limits on it for the sake of community and for a more integrated life.* This, of course, is what marriage or monastic vows entail: the voluntary relinquishing of some measure of freedom—including mobility—for the sake of a common life. Could we extend this commitment to our natural or church communities for a similar reason: to choose depth of relationship rather than a wide but superficial variety of geographical, social, or ecclesial settings?

Even though our vocation does not lie in the literal cultivation of the land, as it does for Wendell Berry, most of us need to settle down somewhere and choose to settle in. Christian community is lived in face-to-face relationships over the long haul, not in the seductive chat-rooms of the web or even in the stimulating but transitory communities of conferences, retreats, or sabbatical years. Authentic community requires shared history—and that is not something that happens overnight. As Robert Bellah noted in his celebrated *Habits of the Heart,* "Where history and hope are forgotten and community means only the gathering of the similar, community degenerates into lifestyle enclave."[9] There is no staying power in lifestyle enclaves, and so we move in and out of them with a kind of promiscuity. When over the years we have not borne one another's burdens and shared each other's joys, what loss is there in leaving when the opportunity presents itself for ca-

---

9. Robert N. Bellah, *et al., Habits of the Heart: Individualism and Commitment in American Life* (New York: Harper & Row, 1985), 154.

reer advancement or the chance arises to live in a more attractive part of the country?

My own quest for community took on a sharper edge when I returned from Africa. While we realized that we could never replicate the natural community of the African village or the all-encompassing seminary community of St. Bede's, we hoped to find something that would approximate, within our limited circumstances, that sense of belonging within the household of faith. And so, after a national job search, we ended up in the same corner of rural, eastern Connecticut where we had already lived for almost twenty years. I took a position as part-time vicar of a little country parish. We moved into the vicarage next to the church and began our experiment in Christian community.

It was not always smooth sailing. In fact, three years into that life I was so disappointed, my dreams for the parish so utterly crushed, my feelings so hurt by groundless suspicions and foolish misunderstandings, that I began to make plans to leave. I would have moved on had not unexpected financial troubles forced me to stay put. Even a half-time salary was better than the non-stipendiary work I had been contemplating. Having resigned myself to working for the paycheck, I decided that I might as well make the best of it. It occurred to me that I might try to love my parishioners as they actually were, not as I hoped they might be.

And then, strange to say, things began to change. An elderly parishioner remarked to me, about a month after what I had thought was an entirely interior shift, "You seem to be more at peace." For reasons I cannot wholly explain, the atmosphere of our life together began to soften. When parishioners realized that I was not leaving and, in the end, did not even want to go, trust emerged. About seven or eight years into that call—just about the time, statistically, that clergy are apt to move—a still more profound level of trust evolved, somewhat instinctively, on both sides. We could take risks and make mistakes and still believe in each other's goodwill and forgiveness. Most of the time we simply got on with living the Christian life together. Sometimes I found out what was going on among my parishioners, but not always. Occasionally I witnessed breathtakingly generous, but often quiet and hidden, acts of mutual care within the parish, combined with a high degree of sensitive responsibility to the community at large. All of it was grounded in a deeply prayed-through Sunday eucharist, which people openly affirmed was the very center of their lives. Luther was surely right when he declared that the church is the church when the word of God is truly preached and the sacraments rightly administered. The rest flows from there. You really don't need much to make it work—except grace, of course.

The strong preference in ascetical literature for geographical stability exists, paradoxically, for the sake of change: not the superficial change of location, but the necessary upheaval of the spirit. Nowadays, pilgrimage is usually more a movement of the heart than a journey to a new site. In the early literature of the desert tradition, the great Abba Moses is reputed to have taught those who came to him seeking a word of direction, "Go, sit in your cell, and your cell will teach you everything."[10] What we need to advance in love of God and neighbor is painfully at hand. The Celtic monks, who sometimes practiced exile as a form of penance, would speak of coming home to the monastery as their "place of death and resurrection."

Where do we find this cell, this community, this place of death and resurrection for ourselves? We North Americans enjoy a certain latitude in our choices, but even our range of options is not absolute. We need to take into consideration the actual circumstances of our lives: our background, our talents, our natural inclinations and holy passions. We need also to take into account the concrete needs around us, and the specific and urgent needs of the church and the world that we may be in a position to address. In our discernment, we must always honor commitments already made, especially to one's family. Children and elderly parents can be particularly vulnerable. We must consider our friends, and not simply toss them heedlessly aside to make our way up the career ladder. Who says we have to take the best job offer or the one that our colleagues might deem an advancement or the position that

<hr>

10. Benedicta Ward, SLG, *The Desert Christian: The Sayings of the Desert Fathers, The Alphabetical Collection* (New York: Macmillan, 1975), 139.

pays the most money? What is "the best," anyway? Doesn't our answer depend on how we define "the good"?

Having found, or in some cases, simply stumbled upon the imperfect community to which we can give ourselves—the place to which "we believe we have been called"—we can let it work on us. Sometimes we will be contradicted, and our wills will be thwarted. But that is the beauty of it! In the church, we can never imagine ourselves better than we are, never suppose that we can do without reconciliation. We come face-to-face with our frustrations and anger, as often as not embodied in—or projected onto—our fellow Christians. What do we do then? Through one situation after another, one distressing encounter after another, God is bringing our true, and often hidden, attachments and desires to our attention. Once we acknowledge these feelings, we bring them before God for judgment and sanctification.

Because many of our interior states are tumultuous or down-right ugly, praying them out can be revealing and humbling. Some of us were taught to be respectful, even polite, in prayer, but excessive deference can lead to distancing ourselves from God under the guise of respect. The fourteenth-century mystic Julian of Nor-wich counsels that it pleases God greatly when a "simple soul comes to him naked, plainly and homely." Julian never loses her sense of holy reverence, but awe before the divine mystery does not keep her from transparency with Christ. Indeed, over and over in her writing she registers amazement that it is the most high God who initiates this familiarity with his creatures. To present our-selves "naked, plainly and homely" in prayer requires confidence that we will be loved no matter our condition. When Julian writes of being with God "naked, plainly and homely" she is using the language of love, suggesting that utter trust in God is the neces-sary prerequisite for divine intimacy.

Some of our unruly feelings and attitudes may simply require confession—contempt, envy, or lust, for example. Other power-ful sensations may be harder to sort out, perhaps because they are connected to our notions of fairness or justice, or because they are linked to older wounds. In any case, naming before God the sur-face thoughts and blatant emotions that are swirling inside us is the clear place to start. Our sense of confusion and helplessness is an ingredient of this prayer, part of what it means to approach God "naked, plainly and homely."

Life in the community of the church, with its ups and downs, its satisfactions and setbacks, offers constant material for prayer, especially if we are attentive to our reactions to what is going on. Reflecting on community life, St. John of the Cross once remarked, "Like stones in a bag we rub each other to smoothness." Inevitably, we will compare the place we are in to the place we just left or the place we thought this was going to be. If we are lucky, we will eventually tire of our inner dialogue with ourselves, our habitual proclivity to size things up. We can let the new situation have its way with us; it can begin to rub our rough edges to smoothness. Usually this will mean letting people rub us the wrong way, as they certainly will from time to time.

There is something to be said for longevity here, for perseverance over time. And so, before we wonder whether we made a colossal mistake in our initial discernment or, after the course of a few years, when we begin to wonder whether it might be time to relocate, some prior questions ought to be faced. Are we merely bored, expecting others to provide intellectual or social stimulation for us? If we have been telling ourselves that "we've done all that we could do here," what do we mean by that particular mantra? Does it mean that our parishioners have resisted our desire to change them? Does it mean that we have preached the round of the lectionary so many times that we cannot come up with a fresh idea? Does it mean that we simply like variety, and that even though the parish programs are working well, we crave some sort of novelty? Are we attempting to avoid a painful situation—an aging congregation with no new, or younger, faces? A financial shortfall? A few difficult personalities? Are we simply ambitious, imagining that someone with our experience should be in a bigger, more prestigious place—never mind that the least coveted positions, in the inner city or amid rural poverty, often require a mature, well-seasoned pastor to stand any chance of growth?

Too often how we relate to our setting reflects the divorce culture of which we are a part. We fail to listen respectfully to what the other is trying to tell us; we lack the determination to weather the rough seasons; we are easily discouraged and give up prematurely. All this bespeaks a lack of confidence in divine grace to renew us and the communities we serve. We end up approaching parish ministry as a kind of strip-mining: we work the surfaces for a while, and when the most easily attainable benefits are secured, simply move on.

There can be sound reasons to seek a new cure or to accept one that we were not initially pursuing. The gospels indicate that our best efforts can meet with failure and, in such cases, we move on and "shake the dust off" our feet. There is no time for blame and recrimination; it is a waste of energy. We can learn from our mistakes, but judgment must ultimately be left for God. The Scriptures also witness to many unexpected—and typically, undesired—calls from God. Fidelity to these vocations—consider Abraham, Jeremiah, Mary, or Paul, for example—entailed considerable hardship and a willingness to be led into an uncertain future. Only later did the grace at work in these calls become apparent.

Discernment is a difficult business, and it is hard to disentangle our tangled motives. Once again, we stand in need of the community of faith to help us gain a measure of clarity. This community might be represented in a few friends who can be trusted to challenge us, or an astute spiritual director—someone who has a bit of critical distance from our circumstance. Our own vocations will not bear fruit, however, unless we replace the question of whether this community is serving my needs with another: "What might I have to give or to learn here?" If we are being called to a new ministry, the reasons should be fairly compelling and have more to do with the work ahead than with dissatisfaction and ennui on our part.

"I struck the board, and cried, No more. / I will abroad,'" confesses George Herbert in his poem "The Collar." The "board" he strikes is a table—perhaps the altar of his parish church. For thirty lines Herbert raves about all the ways he fears he is wasting his life in spiritual pursuits while the open road beckons with its seductions of freedom and pleasure. Then at the end the poem he writes:

> But as I rav'd and grew more fierce and wild
> >   At every word,
> Me thoughts I heard one calling, *Child*:
> And I replied, *My Lord*.[11]

What keeps Herbert from abandoning his calling is the persistent, loving call of God. Like the psalmist, Herbert discloses through his poems his struggle with God. When shortly before his death he handed his poems over to the safekeeping of his friend Nicholas Ferrar, he explained that they contained "a picture of the many spiritual conflicts that have passed betwixt God and my soul, before I could subject mine to the will of Jesus my master; in whose service I have now found perfect freedom." All of us are subject to moods in which we would like to throw in the towel on ministry; short of that, pining for a change of scene can be a tempting fantasy. Herbert's poem reveals a boldness in prayer that is essential for interior progress within any community, whether that of a family, a monastery, or a parish church.

THE DESOLATE VALLEY

*"Those who go through the desolate valley will find it
a place of springs." (Psalm 84:5)*

Most of us enter ordained ministry as idealists of one stripe or another, and that is how it should be. Idealism—or "vision," as the new leadership literature might dub it—has a place in pastoral oversight. However, by our first cure, if not sooner, we find ourselves up against a church or local congregation that does not fully share our vision. Much of the disappointment we feel in our work

11. George Herbert, "The Collar," in *George Herbert: The Country Parson, The Temple,* ed. John N. Wall, Jr. (New York: Paulist Press, 1981), 278–79.

as pastors has to do with what we perceive as the mediocre quality of Christian life in the places we serve, and that is where problems set in. People let us down. We see the possibilities, but the head of some committee or members of the vestry seem stuck in old ways of doing things. They don't seem to "get it"—meaning, they don't understand "my" presentation of the faith or "my" perception of mission.

I have already mentioned that people join a church for all sorts of reasons, some of them reflecting displaced emotional or psychological needs. People who have been geographically uprooted or whose families have disintegrated come to church looking for "community," where their fantasies collide with ours. Members of our congregations may entertain expectations of stability and peace in the church that are wholly unrealistic. Pretty soon they discover that the church also is undergoing change and that members of the church hold a variety of opinions on everything from matters of real moral gravity to the color of the carpeting. Disappointment can lead to rage.

Loving those entrusted to our care can be hard work. Maintaining harmonious collegial relations with other members of the staff, and particularly with other clergy, can be even more of a challenge. We may be discouraged or scandalized by what we take as the shallowness, cowardice, laziness, or stupidity of our colleagues or superiors. Sometimes conflict arises between the rector and associate clergy. In multi-staff parishes and in regional ministries, clergy can feel undermined by their colleagues, although the offense is nearly always unintentional and unwitting. The inevitable friction exposes the meagerness of our inner resources, our impatience and lack of charity. At some point, priests are almost always disappointed by some decision of the bishop or members of diocesan staff; the bishops are disheartened by at least some of their clergy, their attitudes and their antics; and the deacons may well end up disillusioned with everybody.

The breakup of our dreams signals a crisis in our spiritual lives. As a result we can become cynics, perpetually embittered that things are not as they should be. Such cynicism can seep out as low-grade, chronic dissatisfaction with church life, the habitual griping or joyless, mocking humor that all too often characterizes clergy gatherings. Cynicism ensures our emotional and spiritual distance from each other. When this happens, our idealism about what we think constitutes the gospel life, like everything else about us, needs to undergo purification. Our vision for the church has far too much ego mixed in. The shattering of our dreams is really an indispensable part of our salvation. As Dominican theologian Simon Tugwell has wisely observed, "Christianity has to be disappointing, precisely because it is not a mechanism for accomplishing all our human ambitions and aspirations, it is a mechanism for subjecting all things to the will of God. . . . Christianity necessarily involves a remaking of our hopes. And our disappointments are an unavoidable part of the process."[12]

How do we cooperate with this process of having our hopes remade? The danger lies in getting stuck in the extroversion of sadness, allowing ourselves to feel only anger. We mentally rehearse all the ways others are to blame: if only *they* would wise up, act differently, think more clearly, be more "spiritual." But underneath our rage there is grief. There is loss involved in being divested of a cherished ideal. If we cannot, in all honesty, yield some ideal of ours, we may nonetheless have to relinquish its precise embodiment *now* or in the *way* we thought it could work out. Either way, we cannot dodge the grief that hovers just under the surface of our anger and disappointment. We need to mourn, to allow ourselves to be "at a loss" for what to do or say about the situation. New directions may come, but they are not yet evident to us. For the time being, we must occupy a place of spiritual destitution and bereavement.

After a while, we may find the blessedness promised to those who mourn. After the first sharp pangs of loss, after enduring the waves of grief that may wash over us, we may start to notice what we have still been given. After being bitterly disappointed in key parishioners we had counted on (or the rector, other clergy, the vestry, the bishop, Diocesan or General Convention—fill in the blank), we may start to notice how many other people God has set

---

12. Simon Tugwell, OP, *Ways of Imperfection: An Exploration of Christian Spirituality* (Springfield, Ill.: Templegate Publishers, 1985), 1–2.

in our path to provide encouragement. Others may not turn out to be the father or mother figures or the community of our hopes. Eventually, we can release them from that inner demand of ours out of sheer gratitude for all that God has given us instead—so many others, often found on the sidelines of the church, who offer the inspiration and support we need. Becoming disillusioned does not have to make us cynical. Stripped of illusion, we can appreciate, perhaps for the first time, what is really there.

Because we generally lack other markers for achievement, clergy tend to need reassurance from those under our care and over our heads that we are doing a good job. We can be grateful when our efforts are acknowledged. We should be humble enough to accept graciously whatever expressions of appreciation may come our way. If we instead brush off these gestures, we fail to affirm the generosity of others, while denying our own human need for appreciation. Sometimes, however, affirmation simply doesn't come—much of our ministry is hidden from the public eye, and much of it goes unnoticed. Some of our projects meet with failure. The longing many of us harbor to be thought of as the "good boy" or the "good girl"—identities we have never quite outgrown—can compound our disappointment. What might God be giving us through the thwarting of these wishes?

Miriam Pollard, a Cistercian nun living in Massachusetts, shrewdly suggests that we take a more realistic appraisal of our needs and available resources. Interestingly enough, she does not take a fiercely ascetical approach to our crashed plans, but proposes that we neither relinquish our desires nor jump to the conclusion that God alone can satisfy our heart's craving:

> We want everyone to like us always, and get unhinged by the inevitable clashes, corrections, flops, and incompatibilities of a real world. To want, even to need, an uninterrupted, homogeneous, and liberal flow of affirmation is unrealistic.... So when the piers on which we parked our building buckle and slide out from under, their insufficiency only demonstrates that the house is too big for them. We need a foundation proportioned to the load it has to bear. Usually this does not mean, "I require God instead of

creatures." Usually it means, "I require God, and one of the things he will teach me is the practical wisdom of how to accept the human support his providence sends into my life; how to value it for what it is instead of resenting it for what it was never meant to be."[13]

Once we let go of our disproportionate demands that members of the church, whatever their position, conform to our fantasies about what they should do or how they should be, we can appreciate the grace already at work around us. We may begin to notice what good qualities some people actually have; at the very least, we can respect their otherness. Maybe they are not there to please me. Maybe I cannot please some others, either. We are compelled to relocate our sense of worth. Are we only valuable when everyone is applauding? Can we let go of the ways we covertly judge ourselves on the basis of the judgment—real or imagined—of others? God invites us to greater freedom, to a new level of human maturity. Even in middle and old age, it is still a challenge to grow up, isn't it? But surely that is what it means to be ordained as "elders" in the church. It is time to stop insisting that Mom and Dad in their many guises tell us how wonderfully we are doing. When we are ordained, we received authority in the church. Living into that authority, in all humility, can be liberating. We no longer have to be constantly looking over our shoulders for validation.

For authentic community to flourish, as both Wendell Berry and John Zizioulas would remind us in their different ways, geography—specific rootedness—has got to have a priority. We cannot transcend place, much as we sometimes try. It keeps us anchored in the here and now. Yet to sink into our limited and limiting communities (whether of family, neighborhood, or local church) leads, paradoxically enough, to the transcendence of limitation. This is where God offers us the chance to grow in generosity, faithfulness, steadfastness, and love.

---

13. Miriam Pollard, OCSC, *Acceptance: Passage into Hope* (Wilmington, Del.: Michael Glazier, 1987), 115–16.

❧

A COMMUNITY OF DEATH AND RESURRECTION

One Holy Saturday morning a small group met in the church I served, still bare and desolate from the liturgy of Good Friday, to pray the proper liturgy of that day. Holy Saturday is probably the most liminal day in the church calendar, poised as it is between the death and resurrection of our Lord. The Holy Saturday liturgy is a brief service of the Word, with a poignant lesson from the Book of Job lamenting the brevity of life, and New Testament lessons that recall the burial of Jesus and his descent to the dead. After the gospel reading I spoke briefly about the practice of funerary rites, sanctified by the passage of Jesus, his friends and family, through this universal human ritual. My own mother's death three years earlier at the end of Lent was still very much with me, and in my homily, I mentioned that the most difficult moment for me in her funeral arrangements occurred when the undertakers came to remove her body from her bed. She had died at home. In the middle of the night my father and I watched as they gently shifted her body onto a stretcher and carried her down the staircase, out the front door, and into the hearse. It was then that the loss struck home. Three years later, I told them, I still found comfort in recalling that scene in the light of the burial of Jesus, knowing in a deeper way that nothing indeed separates us from the love of God in Christ Jesus. After the Holy Saturday service, some of us stayed on to rehearse the liturgy for the Great Vigil of Easter that was scheduled to begin just before dawn on Easter Sunday morning.

Later that afternoon, I telephoned my father to confirm the time when he would be joining us for Easter Sunday dinner, but he didn't answer. After a few more unsuccessful attempts at reaching him, I telephoned a parishioner who lived in the same condominium complex. Was my father's car in the parking area? She looked out her window and confirmed that indeed it was. My husband and I drove to my father's house, but I already knew.

Upstairs, my father lay peacefully in bed, dead. He had died on "his" side of the bed just as my mother had died on "her" side three years earlier. Notes he kept for himself on his bed table indicated that he had taken his last dose of cough medicine shortly after midnight of Good Friday, so he had been dead for twelve or more hours. After allowing ourselves time to take it all in and to pray by his bedside, the same drill began that we had gone through three years earlier: the family doctor came to confirm his death, and the undertakers came late at night to roll his body gently onto a stretcher, take him down the stairs, and into the hearse. I realized that he had been lying dead in bed when, earlier that day, I had spoken in church of the arrangements for my mother's death. I was being prepared.

The parishioner who was my father's neighbor realized what was happening but didn't intrude. Instead, she called members of the parish leadership to inform them. She also telephoned the parish deacon, who drove to the house to pray with us and console us. A few hours before dawn, we returned to the vicarage, took showers, and prepared for the Easter liturgy. Before the Great Vigil began, the deacon announced to the congregation the news of my father's death. When it came time to preach the Easter gospel, I set aside the text of the sermon I had written earlier that week. Instead, I spoke of the tear-stained and exhausted women at the tomb who, expecting death, instead found resurrection. I had also been to the tomb that morning and, through the Easter liturgy, was now breathing in the fragrance of the Risen Lord.

My father's requiem eucharist took place during Easter Week, and the sense of exceptional grace surrounding his death stayed with me and the parish throughout that Easter season. Meanwhile, I was engaged in the usual round of pastoral duties, including, as it turned out, the birth of a daughter to members of the parish. As was our custom in this parish, we had been praying on Sundays for the expectant mother and father throughout the pregnancy. Since the birth took place over the weekend, I was able to visit and bless the mother and newborn baby in the hospital very early one Sunday morning, and then, with the congregation, later give thanks for this child at the parish eucharist.

It was also our custom, in accordance with a recommendation in the *Book of Common Prayer,* to reserve baptisms for certain feast days that are exceptionally fitting for this sacrament. Pentecost is one of these festivals; happily, a child born or adopted during the Great Fifty Days of the Easter season, as this girl was, might be baptized on that day. It is certainly one of the blessings of parish ministry to accompany families, in the context of the community of faith, through these defining moments in their lives when grace seems so transparent. Sometimes the pastor is part of the couples' conversation about whether to have children and when. Sometimes the pregnancy comes to term easily; sometimes there are problems with fertility or with the adoption process. Sometimes the pregnancy is unexpected or problematic. But in every case the child and parents had been prayed for regularly in the parish intercessions, so when the child arrives, the congregation is fully involved as part of the extended family. Often, the parents express their relief, gratitude, and heightened awareness of their need for continued grace through the Prayer Book's service of Thanksgiving for the Birth or Adoption of a Child, and baptism typically follows on the next appropriate occasion.

That year, we began the Easter season with my father's death, subsumed into the larger mystery of Christ's own death and resurrection. We ended the Easter season with a birth: the natural birth of a child to parishioners, and the new birth of regenerative grace. Baptism, as Paul teaches, is itself a participation in Jesus' death and resurrection. The paschal candle, symbol of the presence of the Risen Lord, burns throughout the Fifty Days of Easter, starting with the Great Vigil, and at baptisms and funerals. That year the presence of the Risen One was almost palpable.

The family whose child was baptized at Pentecost continued their celebration with a picnic for family and friends later that afternoon. My husband and I were invited. There were numerous Italian relatives from one side of the family, lots of good food, and everyone felt the joy of the occasion. When we returned home from the christening party, my husband and I looked at each other and said, "I know what you're thinking. I feel the same way." Without having discussed the topic for years, we had each been stirred that afternoon to end our own childlessness and adopt a baby.

Grace often takes us by surprise. In the bittersweet grief following my father's death, we felt overwhelmed with gratitude for the proximity of my parents during the last ten years of their lives. As distant memories became dislodged from the depths of my mind, I grew conscious of more and more blessings that had come to me throughout childhood. Not that everything was perfect. Our family, like all other families, had its places of sin and sorrow. Yet even these things can ready us for forgiveness and shape compassion in us. What a gift simply to be born, I thought, much less be granted that upbringing. It was a gift to be given away again, even after more than twenty years of marriage, even well into middle age.

About a year later, my husband and I boarded a plane to China to adopt our six-month-old daughter. We had been through another cycle of Lent and Easter with the parish before leaving. That year, the text from St. John's gospel showed up in the lectionary: "Unless a grain of wheat falls into the earth and dies, it remains alone; but if it dies, it bears much fruit" (John 12:24, RSV). In this text, a prelude to the passion narrative, Jesus speaks of his own impending death and glorification. He is also delineating the conditions of discipleship. My father's death, in the context of the Easter mystery and the baptism of a parishioner, had released new life: an abandoned Chinese girl would be given a home; a childless couple would be given a daughter. The parish would have another member, another joyful baptism. And the grace at work here continued to bear fruit in our family, of course, and among members of the parish.

Two years later, a couple visited the parish on a Sunday morning. No one recognized them. Like many people who try the church out, they sat toward the back. This is not an unusual scenario at any parish. What drew my attention, however, was their open weeping toward the end of the eucharist. The strength of their own emotions evidently caught them by surprise and embarrassed them, for they left before the dismissal and final hymn. A parishioner who had been sitting in front of them followed them to the parking lot. "I don't know what's troubling you," she told them, "but this is a place where many of us have shed tears.

Won't you come and join us for coffee in the parish hall?" Although this couple would have many more tears to shed in the years to come, they wiped their eyes and followed her in.

As it turned out, this husband and wife had come to our parish partly because of their own religious background and partly because they had heard from friends that the priest of the parish and her husband had adopted a Chinese child. They, too, were seeking to adopt from China, and had been anticipating an imminent departure. They then encountered an unexpected delay due to various bureaucratic roadblocks. In this time of frustration and dashed plans, they turned to God and the church. Parishioners welcomed them warmly and drew out the story. Before they left, we prayed together in the church that the obstacles delaying the adoption would be speedily and permanently removed. In a few months' time they were back with their baby girl, who looked like a slightly younger version of my own daughter.

In this life, what we see of the resurrection is at most a sidelong glance of it. Occasionally we seem to enter the "thin places," where the veil between quotidian reality and the sublime reality of the kingdom becomes porous and permeable. My father's death on Holy Saturday was such an instance for me. Ignatius of Loyola, that master of discernment, regarded such occasions as "consolations": graces given to encourage us on the path of virtue. Ignatius recommends that we ponder our consolations, asking what we have learned about God and ourselves during these bright moments. In particular, he urges us to recall and to anticipate our "desolations" from this renewed perspective. Consolations may be cherished—after all, they are God's gracious gift—but they cannot be clenched. Inevitably they give way to the whole range of religious and human emotions, some of which are pretty bleak. A true consolation, like any other grace, is best interpreted in hindsight, and its significance is more reliably gauged by its fruits than by its sweetness or intensity. Does it lead us to stronger faith, a more lively hope, a more expansive charity?

⚬⚬⚬

FRIENDSHIP IN COMMUNITY

While ordination sets a priest apart for a distinct ministry in and for the church, our lives are still lived within the context of the Christian community. Can we enjoy friendship with our parishioners and still minister effectively? Conventional wisdom insists that we cannot make friends in the parish, but it seems to me that this assessment of our social situation fails to recognize the multifaceted ways human beings engage in friendship. Of course it is both unwise and unfair to have anyone under our pastoral care serve as our confidante or soul friend. There are limits to what we should disclose to anyone other than a spiritual director, confessor, therapist, spouse, or very close friend. Overstepping that line with parishioners turns the tables on our pastoral relationships, because it means we expect others to care for us in our most acute spiritual need when they should be free to make that claim on us.

However, over the course of a lifetime few of our relationships ever involve such a high level of self-disclosure. Most of us substantially edit our self-revelations to friends, instinctively relating some concerns to one and other personal details to another. There remains a good deal of ordinary human experience that we do share with our parish community: civic concerns touching the town, city, or nation; routine matters of physical health; enjoyment of the arts or other leisure activities; raising children; going back to our college reunion—the places to find common ground are endless. So long as we exercise a healthy measure of prudence in what we reveal about ourselves, we can enjoy a degree of friendship with our parishioners that is emotionally sustaining and practically helpful. They, in turn, may welcome dealings with us that allow them to glimpse our humanity, including aspects of our vulnerability. For instance, I found embarking upon motherhood in middle age a bit daunting—I hadn't changed a diaper since I was a teenage babysitter. Several women of the parish, many of them younger than I, were glad to coach me—when asked—about routine childcare. I remember how reassured I was by our senior war-

den when at the parish coffee hour I described my daughter's recent spell of strange sleep behavior to her. "Oh, those are called
'night terrors,'" she explained, to my relief. "Some of my kids had
them, too. They're harmless and children outgrow them."

Eugene Peterson recommends what he calls the "ministry of
small talk." Since most people most of the time are not in crisis,
we need to be attentive to their actual concerns if we are going to
engage them at all.[14] Grace is for the diurnal as well as the crucial
moments of life. It awaits us in the mundane, and we are more apt
to discover these blessings in the wide spectrum of exchanges that
reveal our common humanity. Underneath the swapping of anec-
dote, news, advice, or humor a more substantial exchange is taking place: the exchange of affection between priest and people.
When a parish exists in a climate of charity, the atmosphere of
love is palpable to all, parishioners and visitors alike, and it colors
all sorts of interactions, even the difficult ones. When we have to
negotiate disagreements, as we inevitably do, it should make a difference in the way we approach one another that we have shared
the eucharist together. It also makes a difference if we have shared
a picnic or concert. The eucharist transforms our human nature
in Christ; time spent together acknowledges and expands it. When
it comes time to participate in the eucharist, these simple, shared
human experiences allow our common humanity to be fleshed
out a bit, and so more fully offered together for the transforming
work of grace.

Many clergy disdain "the ministry of small talk" and avoid the
home visitations or social events where it usually takes place. With
the press of urgent work upon us, engaging in mere chitchat
hardly seems worth the time. It also seems to demean the pastoral
office—no one wants to feel like the recreation director of a cruise
ship, visiting the passengers to make sure everyone is content with
the voyage, bantering about trivialities over cookies and tea. But
the pastoral role here is not that of a goodwill ambassador, although goodwill never hurts parish life. It is a matter of knowing
our people and being willing to be known ourselves. Small talk

---

14. Peterson, *The Contemplative Pastor*, 114–16.

helps establish and sustain relationships, and relationships matter enormously.

When we first come to a parish or when we visit newcomers, our first pastoral responsibility is simply to do a lot of listening. Fortunately, we do not have to be brilliant conversationalists for this to happen, but we do need humility and faith. There is so much we do not know about our flock and a great deal we will never know. We need to assume an inner posture of contemplative waiting. It takes a long time to begin to learn a community's particular history, much less the significant stories of all those who make up a given place. We will know only in part, no matter how long we stay. Since human beings are made in the divine image, there remains an element of mystery, of incomprehensible depth, to them. That will always be true of the people we meet and the communities we serve. People may reveal themselves over time, but they also remain unknowable, even to themselves.

So we approach others with reverence: God has been at work here before we ever arrived on the scene. Belief in what is traditionally called "prevenient grace" helps our natural curiosity along: How has the Spirit been at work in this individual life or in this community? It may take long hours of attentive listening and observing to catch on, but if we are genuinely interested in people, we will learn when and how to move the conversation to a greater depth. Eventually we will get around to the task of interpretation, of discerning the movements of the Holy Spirit or the contrary movements of temptation that are at work. We are there to sow the word of the gospel, but first the soil must be prepared. In the early stages of relationship, we just listen, draw people out, and try to offer understanding, encouragement, or sympathy, as needed. When the crises occur, or when it is time for secrets to be revealed, we might then be trusted with more intimate revelations.

Nowadays, clergy hear a great deal about the place of professional "boundaries" in our work. Certainly a healthy recognition of our need for some privacy and for the claims of personal and family life helps us be faithful Christians and more fruitful ministers of Christ. Obviously, too, we must take precautions to protect the most vulnerable members of our communities, especially children, the elderly, and those with special needs. Nor can we afford to be naïve about even the appearance of scandal or morally compromising situations. Some clergy, however, respond to the call for boundaries by erecting a psychological fortress around their personal and family lives; their parishioners sense that a "Do Not Enter" sign hangs over this dimension of their priest's existence.

This kind of reserve is at odds with the ordination vow "to pattern your life [and that of your family, or household, or community] in accordance with the teachings of Christ, so that you may be a wholesome example to your people" (BCP 532). All facets of our life can and should be an occasion for witnessing to the truth and mercy of God. The ordination rite recognizes the opportunity that we are given in what we are apt to regard solely as our "personal" lives. Naturally, we need a measure of privacy for family life, along with physical solitude for prayer, thinking, reading, and other forms of work or leisure. But privacy is not the same as privatization, roping off some segment of our lives as exclusively ours. Everything belongs to God, even our bodies, as Paul would remind us. It is hard to imagine Jesus' relations with his disciples, or Paul's work with Priscilla and Aquila, if the personal and pastoral were as compartmentalized as they sometimes seem today. When our personal, professional, and family lives are not somewhat open to each other, our experience is diminished and our parishes are weakened.

LEAVING A PARISH

If we have enjoyed a rich community life in the parishes we have served, leaving will be hard for almost everyone. I say "almost" because in every congregation there will be some who will be glad to see us go. If forgiveness needs to be exchanged for grievances or hurts, including those that have been unintentionally inflicted, we should attempt reconciliation. In some cases, misunderstandings can be so deep and complicated that we cannot sort them out; we must leave them before the judgment seat of Christ. But if we have sincerely loved and been loved by most of our parishioners, grieving will be sharp. How do we move through this transition with grace?

What we already know about the process and purpose of grief in other circumstances can help us out. Denial never helps—nor pious verbiage to cover up mixed motives for our departure. Assuming that we honestly believe we are called to another work or if it is time for us to retire, it is best to speak candidly about our own sense of loss, and theirs. Grieving can be an occasion of blessing and thanksgiving if little by little we tell the stories and reminisce together. Grief redirects our attention to the giftedness of relationships, of the church, and of life itself. We never deserved all we were given. How could we ever have guessed we would be offered so much in so many marvelous ways? Thus we are brought back to the Giver.

Because pastoral relationships are constituted in the church and for the church, grief whittles us down to the essentials: the purpose of our common life is our common mission in Christ. Priest and people have distinct roles within that ministry which is, at base, Christ's. Because grief inevitably redefines our sense of reality, the departure of the priest jolts everyone back to the great reality that has not changed: the mission of Christ to the world. That larger purpose held us together while we were graciously allowed to pray and work together at a particular time and in a particular place. It was for the sake of Christ's mission that the priest came in the first place, and that is why the priest is now leaving. It is what the parish will continue to do in the interim and in the future, if it is faithful.

Leaving a parish can be as much a leap of faith as coming to a new one. Thirteen years into my last cure, the School of Theology at Sewanee invited me to enter a search process. I had not been looking for a new position, and at the time I fully expected to retire from the parish that I was serving. Although it had been some years since I had taught in seminary, the prospect of now drawing on my parochial experience and academic training to shape new vocations for parish ministry made sense. Over the course of nearly a year, the search process issued in a definite sense of call, although responding to it involved sacrifices for the whole family. I still "believe I am so called" to seminary teaching, and many unexpected blessings have been ours. Faithfulness is costly, not least to the priest's family, and it is always a delicate and uncertain calculus to determine what we are being asked to relinquish.

After we have left, we continue to hold our former parish in our love and prayers. Many dioceses issue useful guidelines for both priest and parish so they can adjust to their new situation without each other. Clergy should not normally visit their former parish, for instance, not even for social events, until at least a year has elapsed, and not even then without the permission of the new priest. Parishioners must not seek out the former rector for baptisms or weddings. Of course, it would be meddling for the former priest to comment negatively at any time on the new pastor's policies or other parish developments. It is not easy to let go. We are invested in the work we did and we continue to care about the people we left behind: we were invited into their lives and were allowed to be their pastor for a while. The Farewell Discourses in John show Jesus in the process of handing over his disciples to the Father in trustful obedience when the time of his own departure was at hand. These chapters in John invite our meditation as we move, with Christ, into a new reality.

Yet I do not believe a complete break is necessary or helpful. An exchange of Christmas cards, a short note of congratulations or sympathy, an occasional personal visit after some time has elapsed—these things confirm that our affection for our people was always authentic, and not a matter of playing a role that we have now set aside. In his classic work on Christian friendship, the twelfth-century monk Aelred of Rievaulx cautioned that friendships should be dissolved gradually, let loose "stitch by stitch." When a pastor leaves a parish, the new state of affairs should not be treated like a death or divorce. A pastoral relationship has ended, but personal warmth and solicitude will linger. There is no urgent reason to deny these human feelings and many good reasons to give them some play, at least for a while.

Looking back on the many communities of which we have been a part, we know that each one has shaped us significantly. They are all a part of us. Perhaps some memories fill us with pain, sadness, or shame. No doubt there are aspects of our response to situations that call for repentance. Community life in all its manifestations unfailingly exposes our weaknesses. "The whole earth is our hospital," wrote T.S. Eliot. There is no circumstance that cannot conspire for our healing if we let grace work through it. Yet as priests, we also know how grace has worked through us and the people we have served: sometimes predictably (yet wonderfully), as in the sacraments. At other times, grace shows up in pastoral encounters or chance occurrences, leaving us shaking our heads, pondering the faithfulness of God. We can move through the day with a sense of "holy expectation," as the Quakers call their practice of contemplative waiting. Or as the dying priest in George Bernanos's *Diary of a Country Priest* writes, "Grace is everywhere."

CHAPTER TWO

THE SUPPER OF THE LAMB

Celebrating the Holy Eucharist

"Blessed are those who are invited to the marriage supper
of the Lamb." (Revelation 19:9)

ONE EVENING AT a parish supper I fell into conversation
with a visitor. She lived nearby, and I recognized her from my
walks around the neighborhood. After I introduced myself as the
vicar of the church, she cut to the chase. She wanted to know my
reasons for seeking ordination, her curiosity whetted all the more
because I was a woman. Brought up a Unitarian, the Episcopal
Church was foreign territory to her and now she had a chance to
ask a few questions about it. How long had I wanted to be a priest?
What made me desire this ministry? "You must really like people," she surmised. "Well, not quite," I admitted. "That really was-
n't what drew me." Having ventured this far, I decided to tell the
whole truth, come what may: "What I find wonderful about being
a priest is the sense of God's nearness, sometimes when I am with
people as their pastor, and always in the sacraments. In the liturgy,
God is very close—right there, literally, under your fingertips." I
paused and wondered whether I had revealed too much. But she
appeared thoughtful. "Oh, you are so fortunate," she finally

replied. "There was nothing like that in the tradition in which I grew up."

Karl Rahner once wrote: "This is the life of the priest: to dwell completely in the explicit nearness of God."[1] It is almost unavoidable. The ministry of Christ that we exercise is not some pale imitation of what Jesus once did in the remote past. It is not a lesser version of Jesus' ministry that we try to emulate. By the power of the Holy Spirit, Christ acts through us. His ministry is incarnated through our frail flesh. Nowhere is this more obvious and humbling than in sacramental ministry. As we administer the sacraments, we say, "I baptize you" or "I absolve you" or "This is my Body" or "I anoint you." Who is the "I" who is speaking here? It is none other than Christ. Hence in the same meditation Rahner goes on to observe, "By virtue of these words, the priest is completely stripped of power and completely powerful, because they are not his words any more at all, and they are wholly the words of Christ."[2] Anglican theologian Richard Hooker would agree: "Whether we preach, pray, baptize, communicate, condemn, give absolution, or whatsoever, as disposers of God's mysteries our words, judgments, acts and deeds are not ours but the Holy Ghost's."[3] Not because of any personal virtue on our part, but simply as we go about our usual round of activities, clergy have access to that profound experience Paul claims as his own: "It is no longer I who live, but it is Christ who lives in me" (Gal. 2:20). Hence theologians as separated in time as Hooker and Rahner both insist that the priest's words spoken in the sacraments "are not our words any more." What a relief! Who could bear the responsibility of the priesthood if it depended on anything but grace, day by day, moment by moment? Yet Christ speaks and acts through us.

The centrality of the eucharist in the life of the church as well as in the sacramental ministry of a priest makes it natural for us to mark the beginning of a new priest's ministry with his or her first celebration of the eucharist. It is not the first baptism nor the

1. Karl Rahner, SJ, *Meditations on the Sacraments* (New York: Seabury Press, 1977), 68.
2. Rahner, *Meditations*, 65.
3. Richard Hooker, *Of the Laws of Ecclesiastical Polity*, Book V.

first absolution nor the first anointing, but the first eucharist that serves to initiate the new priest.[4] As Austin Farrer observed in a sermon preached at the first mass of a newly ordained priest:

> Just exactly what a priest is, you can see best in the Holy Eucharist. In a great part of the holy action he is, of course, no more than the voice of the congregation. Some of the prayers we say with him, some we let him say for us: it makes little difference. Or again, in receiving the sacrament, the priest is in the same position as any other Christian, receiving the body and blood of Christ. But there is a moment when the priest steps into the place of Christ himself, to do what Christ did, to bless and to break, to present the mysterious sacrifice before God Almighty.[5]

The eucharist has this power to define the priest because it also defines the church. Baptism initiates new members into the church, but baptism is unrepeatable. It is the eucharist that continually brings the church into being, making of it a spiritual organism variously described in Scripture as the people of God, the royal priesthood, the body of Christ, and the bride of Christ.

What is unique about the situation of priests is their vantage point in this process. It is not because we are somehow holier than other Christians, but simply because of our distinctive pastoral ministry that we find ourselves situated in a privileged position to apprehend this grace at work. We have the best seats in the house to notice what is going on—and not only for ourselves but, to a certain extent, for everybody. This is especially true in the celebration of the Holy Eucharist.

Those who preside at the principal act of Christian worship encounter its strong currents of grace at a place of powerful intersection in the liturgy. Praying at the very heart of the church, the priest sees, feels, and enacts the extraordinary transactions occurring between God and the worshipping community. As the

4. Rahner, *Meditations*, 66.
5. Austin Farrer, "Walking Sacraments," in *The Truth-Seeking Heart: Austin Farrer and His Writings*, ed. Ann Loades and Robert MacSwain (Norwich: Canterbury Press, 2006), 140. This sermon was preached on December 22, 1968, seven days before Farrer's death.

liturgy moves through its various phases, priests apprehend these divine actions at close range. The liturgy then reaches its climax in communion—the conjunction of Christ and his church. Priests are caught up in these breathtaking forces, and moved from several directions at once, precisely because it is our ministry to represent both Christ and the church in eucharistic presidency. We feel both sides of it.

What does it mean for the priest to assume this liturgical "double identity" as iconic representative both of Christ and of God's people? Where can we find symbols that might begin to capture this twofold aspect of the priestly vocation, epitomized in eucharistic celebration? How do we negotiate this awesome grace? Such questions warrant a good deal of meditative and theological reflection, for they touch our most profound experiences as priests. Later, we will consider how clergy and worshipping congregations alike might lay hold of these blessings more fully.

A FORETASTE OF THE HEAVENLY BANQUET

There is a wonderful scene at the conclusion of the movie *Places in the Heart* that captures how the eucharist makes present the "age to come." It is Communion Sunday in a little country church in Texas. As the bread and cups are passed down the pews, we see the *dramatis personae* of the film joined in this sacrament of unity: the estranged husband and wife, one of whom has committed adultery; enemies and friends; sinners and the sinned against— the whole motley assortment of personalities who make up small town life. Suddenly we glimpse characters from the opening scenes: the sheriff and the young black man who accidentally shot him, both now dead, the latter a victim of a lynch mob. Taking Holy Communion together, all these now-reconciled characters display the communion of saints, sharing in the eschatological power of Christ's Body and Blood.

In the eucharist we feel ourselves transported to the new creation, the heavenly city. To pray at all involves us in the life of the world to come and the essentially trinitarian shape of all Christian prayer. Because the eucharist is the consummate form of Christian prayer, we are bound to notice those trinitarian dynamics most powerfully at work in the flow of the liturgy. The entire movement of worship is directed toward the Father. The Holy Spirit enables every aspect of this prayer, for only by the prompting of the Spirit can the eucharistic mystery take place at all. And Christ unites the church to himself. Those who have been baptized into Christ, and who thus share in what 1 Peter calls the "royal priesthood," offer themselves, together with the whole creation, to God in union with Christ. Christ gathers us up in his self-oblation. In this transforming union, "Christ unites the faithful with himself and includes their prayers within his own intercession so that the faithful are transfigured and their prayers accepted. . . . The eucharist is the sacrament of the unique sacrifice of Christ, who ever lives to make intercession for us." It is the *anamnesis* of Christ's death and resurrection and "signifies what the world is to become."[6]

The priest's role in the eucharistic celebration is complex. The twofold role of eucharistic presidency becomes apparent as soon as we reflect upon the various "voices" the priest assumes in the course of the liturgy. It is a little like playing two key parts in a play at one and the same time, or in swift succession. Notice how sometimes the celebrant speaks with the voice of the people, articulating and presenting their prayer, as in the Opening Acclamation and the various collects of the eucharist, for example. If the Holy Eucharist were staged as a Greek drama, in these moments the celebrant would fill the part of the leader of the chorus.

But then at certain points in the Great Thanksgiving, the priest assumes another role, as the one who stands in the place of Christ. In the narration of the Last Supper, the celebrant renders the words of institution in the first person. Here the priest stands *in persona Christi,* offering the eucharistic sacrifice, together with the people

---

6. "Eucharist," in *Baptism, Eucharist and Ministry,* Faith and Order Paper No. 111 (Geneva: World Council of Churches, 1982), paragraphs 4, 8.

of God, to the Father. In the Great Thanksgiving, the priest is constantly, although seamlessly, switching roles, now articulating the church's offering of this "sacrifice of praise and thanksgiving," and at other times representing Christ to the gathered community. The corporate voice of that prayer is largely the "we" of the praying church, yet the community also experiences the prayer of Christ to the Father, and the gift of Christ to them, as something flowing through the celebrant. The 1976 *Moscow Agreed Statement* of the Anglican-Orthodox dialogue aptly summarizes the priest's double role here: "The celebrant, in his liturgical action, has a twofold ministry: as an icon of Christ, acting in the name of Christ, towards the community and also as a representative of the community expressing the priesthood of the faithful" (VI. 27).

In actual practice, of course, the two roles cannot be neatly divided, even as we recognize their relative play back and forth in the liturgy. Consider the task of the preacher, for example, a topic that will be considered in greater detail in the next chapter. Preachers are charged with proclaiming God's word to the people: the role of Christ toward the community. In preaching we do not "proclaim ourselves." Our task is rather to discern and then speak God's particular word to a particular community, now. Yet even as we face into that responsibility, we know we must draw upon our human thoughts and words, including our knowledge of our congregation, to convey that message. Preaching continues the dialectic between God and the people. The dual role of the priest is also strikingly apparent during the General Confession. As the priest kneels with the penitent congregation during the confession of sin, she dramatically expresses her solidarity with them in their sinful condition and asks mercy for herself along with everyone else. Yet when the priest rises to pronounce absolution, she embodies that very mercy of God toward the congregation and speaks with the authoritative voice of Christ.

John Zizioulas has noticed the same double role at work in Orthodox liturgy, and for him this dialectic is full of theological significance. The principal trinitarian action during the eucharist consists in the movement between the Son and the Father, as the Son prays through the church, animated by the Holy Spirit. This is one stream of grace the priest may sense while praying the eucharistic prayer. Yet another stream at work between Christ and the church is also mediated by the celebrant. Zizioulas observes that the ancient eucharistic prayers are marked by a complex dialectic. When the bishop enters the church to begin the liturgy, he is greeted as "Christ himself coming into the world in glory—'*Deute, proskunesomen,*' 'Come, let us worship,' which signifies a full identification between the bishop and Christ. Immediately, however, the bishop transfers the prayer to Christ, *as if he were not himself Christ.* Thus in the eyes of the people the bishop *is* Christ; but in his own eyes he is *not*: he prays *to* Christ *for himself,* but to the Father (as if he were Christ) *for the people.*"[7]

It is a dizzying phenomenon. On the one hand, the congregation regards the bishop or priest as a personification, for them, of Christ. On the other hand, the celebrant regards himself as one connected to the people, and so articulates the prayers of the liturgy on their behalf. But that is not the end of it. Because Christ is drawing closer and closer to us in the course of the liturgy, the celebrant winds up praying in Christ, united to Christ, one with Christ—just as the people thought from the start!

The *Moscow Agreed Statement* employs the language of "icon" to describe the priest's ministry. Although this document only speaks of the priest as icon when underscoring the role of the priest as Christ toward the people, there are in fact two—not one—images at play here. I have found it illuminating to meditate on both these images as I try to make sense of the complexities involved in celebrating the eucharist. One of these icons is the "icon of Christ" toward the people; in the western church, the priest has been understood as *alter Christus.*

There is, however, another icon: the one that represents the priestly people. In traditional Orthodox iconography, the royal priesthood of the church is represented by Mary *Theotokos,* particularly in the visual representation of this mystery called "Our Lady of the Sign." This style of icon depicts Mary, arms uplifted in the *orans* position, usually wearing a chasuble—a unisex gar-

---

7. John D. Zizioulas, "The Mystery of the Church in Orthodox Tradition," in *One in Christ* 24 (1988): 298.

ment in antiquity. Within the center of her body Christ is displayed in a golden mandorla of glory: "Behold, a virgin shall conceive and bear a son." The figure of Christ radiates from within her. Such an icon goes beyond the biblical Mary to signify the mystery of the church, the finite containing the infinite, the creature bearing the Creator. The Orthodox interpret this icon as the people of God, the royal priesthood.[8]

When this iconographic tradition has been applied to the eucharist, the celebrant has ordinarily been understood as the *alter Christus,* while the people have been subsumed under the feminine imagery of the church, typologized as Mary or the Bride of Christ. At times, the male-female polarity of this symbolism has been used to justify an all-male priesthood, but such a literalization of the symbols would require for its proper correlative all-female congregations! A more serious problem lies in the rigid ascription of these images to the celebrant on the one hand and the people on the other. While a distinction surely exists between the role of the celebrant and that of the gathered community, the relationship between priest and people is more complex and fluid. Because the celebrant represents not only Christ but also the people, celebrants experience in the action of the liturgy the coming together of these two images—and the graced reality they represent.

The Book of Revelation provides a way to bring the images together. In its final chapters we catch sight of the glory of the heavenly city. To dramatize the indissoluble union between Christ and the church, St. John exploits the nuptial imagery of a wedding feast: we become witnesses to the "marriage" of the bride and the Lamb. It is imagery perfectly adapted to the mystery of the eucharist. Because it is the Risen Lord who breaks bread with us, the Lord's Supper is always our temporal realization of that eschatological feast. Christ and his people are joined—married, if you will—through the eucharist. It is literally our foretaste of the heavenly wedding banquet.

The Lamb image underscores the sacrifice of Christ—the "Lamb who was slain." In the great doxological choruses of Rev-

---

8. Leonid Ouspensky and Vladimir Lossky, *The Meaning of Icons,* trans. G.E.H. Palmer and E. Kadloubovsky (Crestwood, N.Y.: St. Vladimir's Press, 1982), 77.

elation, the Lamb receives worship together with "the one who is seated on the throne" (19:4). By contrast, the figure of the bride is a corporate image—"the holy city, the new Jerusalem," whose bridal gown is made of "fine linen, bright and pure"—linen that represents "the righteous deeds of the saints" (21:2; 19:8). Yoked together through nuptial imagery, these figures convey the intimacy of Christ's union with his church and their mutual fidelity.

In all this rich play of allusion, the eucharistic motif is sounded as well. Amid the heavenly nuptials, an angel charges the Seer: "Write this: Blessed are those who are invited to the marriage supper of the Lamb" (19:9). Indeed, the marriage of the bride and the Lamb *must* take place at a supper, for the only way this marriage could be consummated is by the Lamb's being consumed. On the literal level, after all, the marriage of a bride and a lamb is a metaphysical conceit, impossible to visualize. The Book of Revelation presses these metaphors to the breaking point—the Lamb marries the bride to be absorbed into her being. Here again the sacrificial theme is sounded: it is a slaughtered animal, the paschal lamb, whose destiny is to be eaten and thus disappear in the act of communion. In the Orthodox liturgy this self-emptying is dramatized when the celebrant cuts cubes from the eucharistic bread—significantly called "the Lamb." The same point is made in Episcopal liturgy at the fraction, when the priest proclaims, "Christ our Passover is sacrificed for us," and the people respond, "Therefore let us keep the feast." The Lamb's very nature tends toward communion, and by the Lamb's communion with us we become one with Christ.

In the eucharistic liturgy of the church the priest has typically been seen not only as an icon of Christ vis-à-vis his spouse, the church, but also as one who represents the people before God. Even more remarkably, in the actual experience of praying the liturgy the celebrant may increasingly sense the coming together of Christ and his people, a union they can locate in their own dual role. What image might convey this larger spiritual insight?

There is a painting on the walls of the catacomb of Callixtus in Rome, dating from around the year 200, that may be the earliest representation of the eucharist. On top of a small three-legged table we see bread and a fish. To the left is a man who is placing his hands on the elements in the priestly gesture of blessing; to the right, a veiled woman stands with her hands raised in prayer. She is the bride of Christ, holy church; and she may already be identified with the Blessed Virgin Mary as a type of the church.[9] We cannot know whether the artist consciously wished to endow this eucharistic painting with conjugal imagery, but the painting offers a striking image for our contemplation. For here the symbolic role of the celebrant is not defined solely in terms of "another Christ," but also by the bridal figure of the royal priesthood—both *alter Christus* and *Theotokos,* or God-bearer, as the Fourth Ecumenical Council called Mary. This sense of both distinction and union is something that celebrants experience in presiding at the eucharist.

What is represented iconically in the celebrant takes place in reality for the community at every eucharist: the union of Christ with the church. The eucharistic prayer to the Father, after all, is prayed in union with the divine Son on behalf of the people. The double icon points not to separation but to union, for Christ chooses to identify himself completely with the church. Without this participation in Christ, our prayers in the eucharist, including the Lord's Prayer, would be meaningless or even blasphemous. As it is, the eucharist epitomizes the transformation Paul describes in Romans 8, where he names the "spirit of adoption" as the grace that enables us to cry "Abba! Father!" Human beings can dare to address God the way Jesus does because the Spirit has also been given to us. Christ's prayer becomes our prayer.

Christ's ministry toward the church also passes into the ministry of the celebrant. The act of distributing Holy Communion is at one level simple, almost mechanical, yet its very simplicity leaves us free to notice the flow of divine grace. Christ gives himself completely to this person and to that, some of whom we know and some of whom are strangers to us. The current of grace passes right through us. In letting Christ use us in this way, indeed in feeling him become incarnate in our very bodies, we are only the

---

9. Basil Minchin, *Outward and Visible* (London: Darton, Longman & Todd, 1961), 50–51.

more enriched. The Reverend John Ames, the aging pastor in Marilynne Robinson's novel *Gilead*, puts it this way: "There is a reality in blessing. . . . It doesn't enhance sacredness, but acknowledges it, and there is a power in that. I have felt it pass through me."[10] As both recipient and dispenser of divine grace, we share in Jesus' own experience of having nothing of his own but only what the Father communicates to him.

And so as priests we find ourselves at the intersection of love that flows within the holy Trinity and pours itself out through Christ into the world. When we receive a word for preaching, when we distribute the bread from heaven, when we lay hands for healing and blessing, we are living in Christ. We are not simply imitating Christ or following his example. We are, rather, living inside him. When we pray, it is Christ's Spirit who articulates his prayer in us. When we offer the eucharist to the Father, we are engaging in the Son's self-offering. Aligning ourselves with Christ's gift of himself, transacted through his obedient love, his offering encompasses and transfigures our own small gift of "our selves, our souls and bodies." Inside Christ, we suffer with him the wounds inflicted on his people, his body. Inside him, yet in our spoken words, he intercedes for the whole world and our little corner of it. In him, we sit in glory at the eschatological banquet. All this is the gift of the Father, given through the Son, and realized in the power of the Spirit. To celebrate the eucharist is thus to be situated amid the dynamic, loving, personal energies we call the blessed Trinity.

❧

WITH THE PEOPLE ON YOUR HEART

In a preordination address, Archbishop Michael Ramsey once urged a group of future priests "to be with God with the people on your heart." For parish clergy, or for any pastor who regularly celebrates the eucharist with the same congregation, such a charge

---

10. Marilynne Robinson, *Gilead* (New York: Farrar, Straus and Giroux, 2004), 23.

is not difficult to fulfill. Because of our pastoral office, we are granted access to our people's hearts and all that weighs heavily upon them. Glancing out over our congregation, we are aware of particular joys and troubles—the man recently laid off his job, after fifteen years of faithful service; the woman undergoing chemotherapy; the delight, terror, and exhaustion of the new parents; the quiet joy of someone just returned from retreat. We may also be aware of how sin or grace tends to play itself out in the congregation as a whole: how easily different constituencies in the parish fall into rivalry for attention and resources, for example, or how a new depth of prayer is stirring at the midweek healing service. All these concerns, together with our personal store of aches, desires, and thanksgivings, we bring to any particular celebration of the eucharist. And so, as Ramsey predicts, "You will find yourself, as celebrant at the Eucharist, privileged with a unique intensity to 'be with God with the people on your heart.'"[11]

Presiding at the liturgy bears some resemblance to conducting an orchestra. Before the performance, conductors painstakingly study their texts—the musical score—and know each instrumentalist's part thoroughly. They ponder the nuances of each section, are acquainted with the strengths and weaknesses of their players, and envision the way each musical segment fits into the whole. Rehearsal is crucial. Each musician, even the soloists and those with exposed parts, is intent on performing well, not to draw attention to him or herself, but to contribute to a common endeavor—the creation of an instance of beauty, extended but limited in time.

The liturgy also has its various players: deacon, subdeacon, acolytes, musicians, readers, ushers. The presider, like the orchestra conductor, studies the text and plans the "performance," usually in consultation with those directly involved, making best use of the congregation's gifts and talents. Coaching and rehearsal are needed here, too, even for those blessed with natural aptitudes for liturgical roles. The presider, like the conductor, will always be teaching the players during rehearsal, emphasizing how each part fits into the larger sweep of the liturgy and contributes to its

---

11. Michael Ramsey, *The Christian Priest Today* (London: SPCK, 1985), 16.

beauty. However, during the liturgy itself, the celebrant has her own role to play and trusts that the other players, including the congregation as a whole, are sufficiently rehearsed to carry on without direct supervision. Here the analogy might change to a theatrical play in which it is essential that the celebrant remain in role for the sacred drama to take place.

The celebrant, along with the congregation, receives the gifts others bring to liturgy to enhance our prayer—gifts of reading, singing, and praying. Often the celebrant is not center stage, but attentively listening as the Scriptures are read or intercessions are offered by others. The task here is to embody, through posture and demeanor, such calm and focused attention that we absorb the Word of God ourselves and invite others to do the same. As we listen or pray, we become conscious of Christ's presence— among us, surrounding us, within us. The possibility of discerning it is greatly enhanced by periods of silence and physical stillness at key points in the liturgy: after each reading, after the sermon, after the invitation to the confession of sin, after the fraction, and after all have received Holy Communion and the remaining elements have been either consumed or taken away. There may be other times when a short period of quiet allows the congregation's prayer to sink to a deeper level. Pacing the liturgy to the measure of the Spirit is fundamental. Something as simple as a deliberate pause before praying a collect or beginning the Lord's Prayer can help our concentration. Silence allows us to take in what we have just heard or done and, like the pause between acts in a play or movements in a symphony, it creates space for interior transitions. I once experienced a period of silence after the reception of communion that lasted twenty minutes, the most intense occasion of corporate mystical communion I have ever known. Obviously, a silence of that length is not practical at a parish eucharist, but could we not manage one minute to savor the presence of Christ within us?

Liturgy expresses the grace of what the Orthodox call divine synergy: our working *with God* in creation and redemption. It is a perspective we need to recover, in liturgy and in many other regards, because we tend to ricochet between spiritualities that suggest, at least in practice, that either "it's all up to us" or "it's all up to God." Decades ago, liturgical renewal quite properly sought to restore an active, participatory role to the congregation. In some quarters, however, emphasizing liturgy as the "work of the people" has become a pretext for endless human invention, while correspondingly little attention is paid to liturgy as Christ's gift and action among us.

Participation need not always be extroverted. Having a trained choir offer an anthem or chant a psalm does not mean the congregation has been disenfranchised. In addition to their own singing, listening to sacred music in the context of liturgy can also elicit profound interior participation on the part of the worshippers. Once, after a stunning concert performance of Gustav Mahler's monumental Third Symphony, the man seated beside me, a complete stranger, turned to me and said, "This is better than church." Unfortunately, I knew exactly what he meant! C.S. Lewis's Screwtape assures his diabolic protégé that hell is filled with constant noise. Heaven, on the other hand, enjoys silence and music—an image Lewis may have taken from the celestial worship of the Book of Revelation.

To serve regularly with a deacon, as I once did, is a singular blessing. For the deacon, as for the priest, the eucharist in many ways defines vocation, even in cases where the deacon's center of ministry is found in secular employment. The liturgical functions assigned to the deacon—reading or singing the gospel, leading the prayers of the people, inviting the congregation to the confession of sin, setting the holy table at the offertory, performing the ablutions, assisting at the administration of Holy Communion, and issuing the dismissal—all these actions define the deacon's ministry as a whole because liturgy is more than a sequence of ritual acts. The deacon stands among us as an icon of Christ the servant.

For over a decade I presided at a parish liturgy with a deacon at my side. Week after week the love of God for the world came home to me as he led the parish intercessions and the confession of sin. Like most Episcopal parishes, we used one of the prescribed forms for the prayers of the people found in the *Book of Common Prayer*, and like most parishes, we augmented the general biddings with local names and concerns: for Sam, in his bereavement; for Will and Alice, as they prepare for holy matrimony; for safe travel for Nell and Howard; and so on. We never stopped praying for peace in the Middle East and other troubled areas of the world. Most parishes have similar lists, changing just a bit Sunday by Sunday.

What gave these prayers poignancy for me and for the congregation was the deacon who was leading them. Most deacons in my diocese do not serve parishes during the week but are engaged in some form of service profession: as nurses, for example, or directors of homeless shelters and soup kitchens. The deacon at our parish was a psychological counselor who specialized in working with sex offenders. The nature of his work required strict confidentiality, and he rarely spoke of it even in general terms. Most of the time we all just knew it was there, as a sort of backdrop to our life together as a Christian community. Other deacons had ministries to other "untouchables"—people with AIDS, prostitutes, prisoners, drug addicts, the homeless, the destitute, the elderly, and the dying. I could not say, exactly, what went on in our deacon's soul week after week as he presented our pleas to God. But I could not help feeling that it must have been significant for him, as it was for the rest of us, that one who, like Christ, did not hesitate to associate with those our society considers among the most contemptible of sinners was leading our intercessions. "Blessed are the poor in spirit": deacons know this paradoxical blessing. We pray best when we pray out of our interior destitution, our poverty before God. It was the publican, not the Pharisee, whose prayer Jesus commended: "God, be merciful to me, a sinner!" Likewise, it was the deacon who, on his knees, began our confession of sin. The altar ministry of the deacon was then but the liturgical expression of this ministry of humble, helpful service: waiting on tables, competently and reverently. The deacon prepared the table and restored it to order after Communion, always ready to give way and to stand to the side.

The deacon, of course, dismisses the congregation at the conclusion of the liturgy—an action, like the other liturgical responsibilities of the deacon, that is freighted with meaning. In some simplistic interpretations of the eucharist, a sharp distinction is drawn between the gathered faith community and "the world." When this notion is in the air, the dismissal is interpreted—and often issued—as a clarion call to action, a rousing whoop for mission. The world, however, is not outside the eucharist, but in it: "The world, to which renewal is promised, is present in the whole eucharistic celebration." In the course of the liturgy, the congregation prays for particular communities, the nations, and the whole creation, finally offering it all to God in the context of eucharistic transformation. The eucharist itself is the most powerful divine action for the redemption of the world: "The eucharist involves the believer in the central event of the world's history."[12] It is not a mere feeding station for the troops before they march out to win the world for Christ through their own labors.

The deacon's presence in the liturgy reminds us that the world is not outside, waiting for us to save it, but inside, actively loved by God and in the process of being redeemed. Through the eucharist, we participate in this divine love and action. The deacon's liturgical role, like his or her ministry apart from the liturgy, has to do with this interface between God and the world. Hence it is the deacon who proclaims the gospel—the "Holy Gospel of our Lord Jesus Christ"—given because "God so loved the world." The deacon issues the dismissal so we might continue to live eucharistically, so our prayer and day-to-day activities suffer no rupture between them, but are embraced as a seamless whole.

Dwelling in the Nearness of God

For many clergy, liturgy was the lure with which God wooed them into the church and maybe even into the priesthood. At a purely natural level, liturgical symbols drawn from the premodern world connect us in healthy ways to our own psychic depths and ancestral history. The rites of the church employ simple agricultural

---

12. "Eucharist," in *BEM,* par. 23 and 20.

products—bread, wine, oil—and play with natural contrasts—darkness and light, fire and water—that people have been using in worship for millennia. These ancient roots are the anthropological foundations of Christian worship: they function like the pagan shrines upon which many a Christian church was constructed, offering silent testimony to the way grace builds upon nature.

The church year allows us to move through its seasonal variations with its satisfying rhythms of continuity and change. In the northern hemisphere at least, the natural oscillation between diminishing and lengthening days centered around the winter and summer solstices parallels the imagery at work in the liturgical seasons, adding depth of perspective to our horizon. And then liturgical time takes a great leap, carrying us into another plane of reality with seasons such as Advent and the weeks after the Epiphany, or feast days such as the Annunciation or the Transfiguration. With its round of seasonal or festal lections and its distinctive hymns, colors, and customs, the liturgical year repeatedly immerses us into the fullness of Christ. Even the commemoration of the saints' days invites us into communion with him as part of the closer fellowship with those who belong to Christ. The church calendar thus frames the liturgy that is at the heart of our life in Christ, the place in which we most regularly discover "the explicit nearness of God."

Or at least we once did. For many clergy, the liturgy can start to feel more and more like a service for others, but not a source of renewal for themselves. Many of us do not feel quite nourished by the liturgy, even though there is some satisfaction in feeding others with word and sacrament. Sunday can seem a bit flat, or just plain exhausting. Over time, we notice that the liturgy feels more like a performance than a prayer. Maybe it rushed by, and we end up feeling cheated. Perhaps there were too many Sunday morning crises leading up to the liturgy for us to concentrate on its grace. There was an abundance set before us, but it was more than we could absorb.

We need to be realistic about what might set the stage (and liturgy is, after all, a form of sacred drama) to help us engage in it at a depth of spirit. Just turning up the volume, as some clergy do to work up some enthusiasm, will not work. In the long run it will add to our fatigue and to the congregation's; even worse, it fails to address the roots of our spiritual weariness, malaise, and hunger, while distracting us from our condition. The first step, obviously, is to acknowledge the problem we face and then ask the Spirit, "the Lord, the giver of life," for guidance. How might the Spirit be contriving to blow a fresh wind our way? Many of us are infected with a low-grade, chronic despair that assumes nothing can ever change. We imagine we are saddled indefinitely with a schedule and set of expectations that leave no room to breathe. How might the Spirit release us from the bind we are in, and how will we have the courage to cooperate?

Praying the eucharist is an arduous spiritual exercise. Because it contains a wealth of meaning and a veritable banquet of grace— as many as three Scripture lessons and a psalm, the preached word, a profession of faith, intercessions, a confession of sin, the offering of the Great Thanksgiving, the reception and administration of Holy Communion—we cannot take it all in unless we are prepared for it. In the ascetical discipline of a bygone era, the faithful fasted prior to Holy Communion; today, the eucharistic fast we require is not so much an abstinence from food as a fast from mental overcrowding. We need to hollow out some interior space to hear and receive God's word. If we are not to be frustrated by the liturgy, upset that it somehow just washed over us, or annoyed with ourselves because we were too tired or preoccupied to concentrate, we need to find strategies to approach the liturgy with the relaxed receptivity all prayer requires.

Some of the most prayerful liturgies I have attended have been celebrated in monastic houses. It makes eminent sense to celebrate the eucharist in the context of silence: a silence that reigns from Compline the night before until after breakfast the following morning. We are as prepared as we ever can be for the awesome mystery of the eucharist after we have prayed the morning office and then spent some time in personal prayer and meditation. In many monastic communities, this period of silent prayer lasts for about an hour. Or I recall my experience of worship at the South African seminary in the Transkei where I taught for a term. Each day began at 6:30 in the morning in the chapel with the other members of the faculty and our students. We sat together in silent meditative prayer before the eucharist began at 7 o'clock. Later on, in some of our classes, we talked about how we used that period of silence. Everyone found it a struggle at least some of the time. In silence we face ourselves, with our distractions, preoccupations, resentments, and all our inner turbulence—and we face God. Yet for all our inner thrashing about beforehand, those celebrations of the eucharist had an extraordinary power to them because of our grounding in silent prayer. The spontaneous intercessions of the community came right out of the depths. They are among my most precious memories of that remarkable year.

Parishes are neither monasteries nor seminaries. The schedules and disciplines of both these residential communities cannot be directly transferred to a parish. What I have learned from my association with monastic communities over the years is something more fundamental: the necessity of living deliberately. The Society of St. John the Evangelist, for example, maintains the traditional round of the monastic offices in choir, a commitment to personal prayer and meditation, and an active pastoral ministry. I know the monks well enough to know they sometimes feel stretched by the multitude of demands and expectations placed on them, just as parish clergy do. Yet they keep asking themselves basic questions: What is our deepest calling? How can we arrange the details of our personal and community lives to honor that vocation? How do we make ends and means fit together?

The Catechism names our common, definitive calling when it states that "the mission of the Church is to restore all people to unity with God and each other in Christ" (BCP 855). Although people come to church with an array of motives, most of them are cognizant of their hunger for God and their need for reconciliation. Many sincere seekers, however, know nothing of the Christian contemplative tradition. Rather than turn to the parish church, they are more likely to seek out an ashram, a Zen meditation hall, or some form of New Age practice in their spiritual quest. We clergy do not need to tailor our liturgies to a new market of spiritual consumers, but to discern the uncomfortable promptings of the Holy Spirit. What is underneath the restlessness and voracious consumerism of our culture? What is lurking beneath our own dissatisfaction and edginess? At the eucharist, Christ speaks his living word and sets a table: "Ho, everyone who thirsts, come to the waters; and you that have no money, come, buy and eat!" (Isaiah 55:1). We are offered our heart's desire.

Yet our Sunday morning schedules seem designed to undermine Christ's promise and invitation. Martin Smith writes:

> It seems almost too much to ask for, and yet I dream of a church equipped to help us resist the tyranny of clock time. Such a church would make room for forms of worship designed to take away the pressure of watching the clock, worship that encourages us to enter a different level of awareness and receptivity, worship that opens us to a sense of eternity. It is a lot to ask for, because our current regular forms of worship are bound by rigid schedules. In many parishes virtually every service must be squeezed within one hour because we all need to be going on to the next thing. And the pace of many of our liturgies is quick-fire, as if we had to keep it going in order to get it over with in time.[13]

Many clergy are apt to say, "If it doesn't happen on Sunday morning, it doesn't happen." And so we fill every available space with everything from worship to coffee hour to church school for children to adult classes to Bible study to committee meetings. And that's just the morning. Is it any wonder that we arrive for the eucharist breathless and maybe out of sorts? What is happening on Sunday morning that is really important? Worship is the "one thing needful." We have to clear sufficient space so we can receive its grace. A "sense of eternity" cannot open out for us when we are rushed and distracted. If we set the liturgy, together with its necessary prayerful context, as our highest priority, and engage in it with loving attention, other things fall into place. The eucharist has power to enlarge our vision, to alter our perspective. We can then see what other parish activities might accommodate them-

---

13. Martin L. Smith, "Clock-Watching," in *Compass and Stars* (New York: Seabury Books, 2007), 48–49.

selves to the Sunday schedule. Perhaps some functions can be let go or moved to midweek. If parishioners found their Sunday parish eucharist a window into eternity, an occasion to enter a "different level of awareness and receptivity," they might well be willing to return on a weekday for other matters. Or those other matters might fade in significance.

Eucharistic preparation entails a willingness to undergo conversion—again. The invitation to the General Confession in Rite One says it well: "Ye who do truly and earnestly repent you of your sins, and are in love and charity with your neighbors, and intend to lead a new life, following the commandments of God, and walking from henceforth in his holy ways: Draw near with faith . . . " (BCP 330). We will be agitated during the liturgy or complain that we "got nothing out of it" if we enter it with anything short of a willingness to surrender our lives to God on the spot. Even if we have just quarreled with our spouse that very morning, even if getting our children ready for church has been exasperating, even if we arrive at church to find the furnace shut down in winter or the plumbing blocked up, even if we are feeling utterly miserable and unprepared, we must hand ourselves over to the cleansing and recreative hand of God: "I will go to the altar of God, to God my exceeding joy" (Psalm 43:4). We trust that God will accept us "naked, plainly and homely."

The spirituality of the *Book of Common Prayer* presupposes self-examination, repentance, and the confession of sin. The much-neglected Exhortation in the Prayer Book succinctly sets forth the New Testament teaching on eucharistic discipline. The brief pause before the General Confession is not the time to begin this exercise. Some make daily self-examination an aspect of their spiritual discipline, noting each day's places of tension, weakness, and shame. Others spend this searching time with God less frequently, but probably at least once each week we ought to take stock of our state before God. What have we been hiding from ourselves and God? Where do we feel blocked and defeated? What do we want to offer for God's mercy, healing, and transforming grace? How are we being called to participate in that process? Is our confession sufficiently articulated in our prayer or do we need to seek out another priest for the rite of reconciliation?

Our interior preparation is then matched by careful preparation of the external instruments of liturgy. Our prayer will be more centered if we take time the day before, or at least well in advance of the liturgy, to make sure that everything that pertains to the celebration is in order: that our Prayer Book, hymnal, and Altar Book are marked at the appropriate places, for instance. If we wait until a few minutes before the scheduled liturgy for this task, we will be stressed by the constraints of time, and we risk becoming irritated if we discover something is amiss. Naturally, we would undermine the ministry of sacristans or altar guild if we redo all their work, but the responsibility does fall to us as presiders to make sure everything is in place so that we will not distract our congregation by flipping through pages at the altar or prayer desk, looking for the next prayer or hymn. As celebrants, we are there to pray with such attention, clarity, physical composure, and devotion that our entire bearing draws the congregation to pray. Everything in us contributes to, or detracts from, our prayer— our minds, our hands, our bodies. Erect posture, with both feet on the floor when sitting, hands calmly placed on our thighs, is of vital importance in using our bodies to keep our spirits in relaxed, not strained, attentiveness. The prayerfulness of the priest, deacon, and other altar ministers silently invites the congregation to pray with their whole selves as well.

One of the most perceptive and eloquent writers on the subject of priestly spirituality was a Church of England laywoman, Evelyn Underhill, who was well aware of the influence the priest's own spiritual life has on the parish. A scholar of prodigious learning and remarkable holiness, Underhill served as a spiritual director and retreat leader for both clergy and lay people at a time when women rarely exercised such pastoral ministry. When in 1936 she addressed the Worcester Diocesan Clergy Convention, she spoke to that assembly about the prayer of priests, including their role in the eucharist, and her words continue to have striking relevance to the priestly vocation:

The spirit of prayer is far more easily caught than taught.... The priest who prays often in his own church, for whom it is a spiritual home, a place where he meets God, is the only one who has any chance of persuading his people to pray in *their* own church. True devotion can only be taught by the direct method. The mere presence and atmosphere of a pastor who does what he says, and does more than he says—for whom prayer is the central reality of his life—who comes early into his church to make his preparation before the Eucharist, is absorbed in what he is going to do, does it with recollection and love, and returns to the church to make his thanksgiving among those to whom he has given the Bread of Life—this teaches prayer.[14]

Once our immediate preparation is complete, the liturgy can be anticipated with yearning and joy. As an aspect of our pastoral oversight, the unhurried preparation we have secured for ourselves needs to be available for our parishioners as well. At the very least, our parish churches should be quiet enough that people who want to pray before the liturgy can do so. Nothing is more inimical to the spirit of prayer than the chatter of ushers, choir members, altar guilds, and people sitting in the pews before the service. It needs to be a corporate discipline of every parish to allow holy space for prayer on Sunday mornings. A brief notice in the bulletin, set in the larger context of hospitable welcome, can cue visitors. For instance, we could head the order of service with a phrase like "Upon entering the church, we remain in prayerful silence," as one parish has done. If people cannot pray quietly in their own church, where can they pray?

The same may be said for the atmosphere in sacristies prior to the eucharist, where too often pandemonium reigns. It is not really possible for celebrant, deacon, assisting clergy, acolytes, and other altar ministers to pray the liturgy when they feel they have been catapulted into it. It is possible, even in small parishes where there is a minimum of room to vest, even when there are lots of

---

14. Evelyn Underhill, "The Parish Priest and the Life of Prayer," reprinted in *The Mount of Purification* (London: Longmans, Green & Co., 1960), 265–267.

small children nearby in the Sunday school or nursery, for the sacristy or vesting area to be a place of reverent quiet for at least ten minutes before the liturgy begins. Pastors need to set guidelines that will liberate them and everyone else in the sacristy from the burden of being chummy. They can make it clear that except for emergencies the sacristy is off limits to anyone other than the altar ministers for that brief period. There is a place for small talk and socializing in parish ministry, but it is not now.

As spiritual teachers, we are entrusted with the task of explaining the purpose of silence as a means of more acute listening to God. It helps us set our habitual drivenness aside in order to be more available to God. "Silence is a necessary context for our coming to know God truthfully," observes Samuel Lloyd. "To probe the meaning of the silence of prayer is to explore the mystery of God's nature and ways with us."[15] We will discover that some occasions present themselves naturally for this kind of teaching: training new acolytes or ministers of Communion, for example, or inquirers' classes that delve into the sacraments and liturgy. From time to time, opportunities will arise for instructing the congregation as a whole on the meaning and use of the silences that punctuate the liturgy. Some members of the congregation may at first resist "wasting time," but once the rich potential of silence is elucidated and experienced, these objections may melt away. When periods of silence are incorporated into the regular rhythms of worship, people stop feeling they are being rushed through the liturgy and can savor its many blessings. Their sense of "unity with God and each other in Christ" is significantly strengthened.

Parishioners who come to the early eucharist because they claim to find it more "peaceful" or even more "prayerful" have something to teach us. Their preference might signify a hunger for personal prayer and meditation, a longing for a close relationship to God without knowing what to do with these aspirations. Parishes seldom offer teaching about the Christian contemplative tradition of *lectio divina* (meditation with Scripture), simple forms of contemplative prayer, or exposure to the classics of Christian

---

15. Samuel T. Lloyd III, "The Silence of Prayer," in *Sewanee Theological Review* 35:2 (1992): 164, 159.

mysticism. The desire for a "quieter" Sunday eucharist might also indicate that people feel bombarded with stimuli at the later service. Although clergy frequently charge that members of the early congregation are avoiding involvement with the parish and its members, these early bird congregations are often composed of the most faithful members, who generously give themselves for service.

Some parishes respond to the desire for more contemplative depth in the liturgy by offering "contemplative eucharists" outside of the usual round of Sunday worship. Here protracted periods of meditative silence can be enjoyed, and music, if any is used, usually consists of simple, easily learned, repetitive melodies, such as Taizé chants, that instill a sense of peace and openness to God. Whenever possible, using a low table for an altar, with the people sitting around on cushions or meditation benches, enhances the setting. Such liturgies can be significant occasions for people to realize both the simplicity and overwhelming gift of the eucharist.

I believe it is a mistake, however, to offer special contemplative eucharists in order to maintain hurried celebrations on Sunday. For the vast majority of our parishioners, the place they begin to learn prayer is at Sunday worship. As Underhill reminds us, "The spirit of prayer is more easily caught than taught," and Sunday morning worship offers the most obvious place to catch it. While personal and corporate prayer differ in both their situation and their methods, developing the capacity to use silence is common and necessary to both. The very heart and soul of our pastoral responsibility to shape our parishioners in their life in God is at stake, for "liturgy has immense formative power."[16]

With a contemplative approach to praying the liturgy, we are more apt to notice the ways Christ is present to his people and binding them to himself. When we are "with God with the people on our hearts," we may become increasingly aware that the love we bear our congregation is more than just our own; our hearts have been widened to encompass something of the measure of Christ's love. It is *Christ* who is with God with the people

---

16. Christopher Cocksworth and Rosalind Brown, *On Being a Priest Today* (Cambridge, Mass.: Cowley Publications, 2002), 76.

on his heart—praying for them, with them, and in them. As the author of the Epistle to the Hebrews puts it: "He holds his priesthood permanently, because he continues forever. Consequently he is able for all time to save those who approach God through him, since he always lives to make intercession for them" (7:24–25). To be with God with the people on our hearts is thus to find ourselves plunged into the intercessory prayer of our eternal high priest.

In the course of celebrating the Holy Eucharist, we will diminish this sense of Presence for ourselves and our congregation if we direct the flow of energy toward ourselves as personalities. For example, when celebrants begin the liturgy or their sermon with a hearty "Good morning!" they no doubt mean to convey warmth and welcome, but end up placing themselves rather than God in the spotlight. The banality of such secular greetings, when inserted into the liturgy, both trivializes our religious language and diverts attention from the Holy One among us. It suggests that the cleric rather than Christ is the host at this meal. By contrast, the Opening Acclamations of the *Book of Common Prayer* direct our speech toward the praise of God right from the start, and establish the ecstatic, doxological tone of liturgical prayer.[17] The authentic liturgical salutation of priest and people—"The Lord be with you. And also with you"—can thus be exchanged as a reciprocal blessing. In the prayer of the liturgy these blessings are actualized: the Lord is indeed with us and within us.

"Blessed are those who are invited to the marriage supper of the Lamb." The communion of Christ and his church takes place at every eucharist. Those who preside at this liturgy, who are privileged to speak the prayer of Christ on behalf on the entire priestly people, cannot help sensing this grace with piercing vividness. What the saints and mystics of the church have known—that we are utterly taken up into Christ—is available to us at every eucharist. As Evelyn Underhill writes of the eucharistic celebration:

17. What Hans Urs Von Balthasar maintains about the content of dogmatic theology, that its very content lies in a "double and reciprocal *ekstasis*—God's 'venturing forth' to man and man's to God," is all the more true of the prayer from which theology springs. See his *Seeing the Form*, vol. 1 in *The Glory of the Lord: A Theological Aesthetics*, trans. Erasmo Leiva-Merikakis (San Francisco: Ignatius Press, 1982), 126.

Here every priest is allowed to share the central religious experience of the saints; comes up to the frontiers of the supernatural, stands in that Upper Room whose window opens towards Calvary, commemorates in awe and joy the great movement of charity of which the Church was born, and renews the sacred action in and through which the divine self-giving is set forth, the soul is nourished, and the Church and her Master meet.[18]

---

18. Underhill, "The Parish Priest and the Life of Prayer," in *The Mount of Purification,* 260–261.

SERVING THE WORD

Prayer for Preaching

"We will devote ourselves to prayer and to serving the word."
(Acts 6:4)

PREACHING TAKES PLACE in the context of liturgy. It is
an action within the larger action of worship. Preaching should
not be confused with prayer, however, for it is speech addressed
not to God, but to the worshipping congregation. Yet poised as it
is between the reading of Holy Scripture and, usually, the celebration of Holy Communion, preaching prepares the congregation for prayer, for their participation in the sacred mysteries. "You
have already been cleansed by the word that I have spoken to you,"
Jesus assures his disciples, and preaching should do that, too. It re-
freshes the cleansing, transformative grace of baptism. It cultivates
our ongoing conversion to Christ. It forms in us the perspective
of the gospel. It sharpens our vision of the kingdom of God. All
this means that the preacher must have access to deep wellsprings
of grace. Excellent books are available to coach the novice or seasoned preacher in the art of the homily. My concern here, though,
is not to discuss homiletic techniques, but rather to uncover the
grace we need to prepare and deliver our sermons.

A couple of years after I had returned to parish ministry as my primary vocation, a friend of mine asked me what I found most difficult about it. Without a moment's hesitation I replied, "Preaching every week." I surprised even myself by the vehemence of my response. After all, parish ministry entails all sorts of challenges, and words usually come fairly easily to me. But it isn't verbal aptitude, shrewdness, or even experience and practice that makes the preacher. Preaching is a demanding spiritual exercise, requiring discipline, study, prayer, and hard work. And preaching is, or can be, an extraordinary experience of the grace of God working in and through every facet of our humanity. Because preaching entails public performance, it can become an occasion for heightened self-consciousness, anxiety, and personal vanity. But preaching can also be a powerful instance of grace, as much for the preacher as for the congregation—perhaps even more for the preacher. For preaching demands our dependence upon grace. It begins with the distressing awareness of our chronic lack of inspiration, the meagerness of our inner resources, and requires us to stand before God, waiting and expectant.

If you preach regularly, then preparing, worrying about, writing, and delivering sermons occupies a significant part of your workweek. It is a strain to preach every week, year in and year out. Even those who serve in multi-staff congregations, where a rotation of preaching assignments is shared among clergy, feel the weight of this responsibility. And yet it would be even harder to keep silent: "Woe to me if I do not preach the gospel!" cried St. Paul. The urgency of the Word seeking to be spoken into the world is something we feel quite sharply.

The vocation to preach is an essential ingredient of the pastoral calling. Those who feel themselves called to the priesthood but who shy away from preaching and teaching are captured more by a sacerdotal archetype than by a calling to the real work of priesthood. Preaching serves as an extension of pastoral care and oversight as we bend our efforts to shape the community of faith through the preached word. Over time, both liturgy and preaching inform the spiritual grounding and theological outlook of a community. Congregations that are regularly exposed to sound preaching tend to bring a developed sense of quiet anticipation, a notable stillness and attentiveness, to the sermon.

Yet within this publicly enacted and community-shaping ministry, preaching still seeks to address each member of the congregation personally. As Thomas Oden writes, "The preached word addresses the whole community, yet by this means hopes to penetrate the heart of each individual in the community as if alone before God."[1] Pastoral conversations have a way of following upon sermons that have managed to breach defenses, thrown new light upon old dilemmas, or touched hidden places in the soul. Preaching is also evangelistic, with power to draw those on the margins of the church, as well as unbelievers and skeptics (including the unbeliever and skeptic who resides within each of us), closer to the gospel. In his *Confessions,* St. Augustine relates how he was first drawn to listen to the preaching of St. Ambrose out of a professional interest: he visited the cathedral of Milan simply because he wanted to observe another highly esteemed rhetorician at his craft. Repeated exposure to Ambrose's preaching, however, wore down Augustine's resistance to Christian teaching, unraveled his intellectual difficulties, and brought him to faith.

SPEAKING THE WORD

"And Jesus was speaking the word to them." (Mark 2:2)

The gospels suggest that preaching and teaching, along with healing, constituted the main ministerial activity of Jesus. Jesus is almost constantly engaged in a ministry of the word—with one word for the crowds that followed him, another for his closest disciples, and still another for Nicodemus, the Samaritan woman, Zacchaeus, or Martha of Bethany. In much the same way, our ministry of the word is not restricted to the pulpit, but takes place

---

1. Thomas C. Oden, *Pastoral Theology: Essentials of Ministry* (San Francisco: HarperCollins, 1983), 130.

in classes we teach, in pastoral counseling, at the hospital bedside, during home visitations, at the school board meeting, in the guidance we offer parish committees, in conversations with all and sundry. There is a close correlation between our handling of the word in public discourse and in private exchanges, between sermon proclamation and pastoral conversation. Nevertheless, it is in preaching above all that we feel most acutely the pressure to speak God's word, if we can, with clarity and power.

The central claim of preaching on the apostles is evident throughout the New Testament. The synoptic gospels show Jesus sending out the Twelve, and later the Seventy, charged with a ministry of healing and proclamation. When Paul speaks of his own apostleship, he does so in terms of a commission to preach. He insists that Christ sent him only "to proclaim the gospel" (1 Cor. 1:17), and his letters to the churches continue to proclaim the mystery of Christ's death and resurrection and its ramifications for the church. The conclusion of 2 Timothy portrays Paul near the end of his life and ministry. Anticipating his imminent death, Paul hands over the legacy of the gospel to Timothy, his younger colleague in ministry, and urges him to miss no occasion for proclaiming the gospel: "Preach the word, be urgent in season and out of season, convince, rebuke, and exhort, be unfailing in patience and in teaching" (2 Tim. 4:2, RSV). The lines between preaching and teaching seem to blur here, for the energy of the gospel, with its dual word of judgment and comfort, is able to quicken public preaching, private exhortation, and everything in between.

Early in the Acts of the Apostles, as Luke describes the first instances of apostolic preaching after the resurrection and the formation of the incipient church, he presents an incident that is telling, I think, both for apostolic identity and for the conditions necessary to the ministry of the word. The event is the "institution of the Seven," traditionally associated with the inauguration of the diaconate, when the apostles decide to devote themselves "to prayer and to serving the word" (Acts 6:1–4). This is a fascinating episode from several different angles. We see the church, even at this early stage of development, recognizing that her ministry requires a variety of gifts and services. The Hellenists had complained that their widows were being shortchanged, suggesting a divisive cultural tension between the two groups. In the face of this crisis, nobody suggested that the ideal of practical sharing in the community had simply become too contentious and so had outlived its usefulness. For the Jerusalem church as Luke portrays it, "community of goods" flows directly from the grace of baptism, from a discipleship characterized by a common life shaped by the "apostles' teaching and fellowship, the breaking of bread and the prayers" (Acts 2:42). The fair distribution of food within the community put flesh on this spiritual fellowship and was a necessary concern of the church. The apostles recognize that this ministry must continue but on a new footing: it has to be exercised in a manner above reproach. At the same time, however, the apostles realize that they are not called to this sort of work themselves. Instead, they exercise their pastoral oversight of the community by calling everyone together for their collective wisdom to resolve the problem. The Twelve use this occasion to define their distinctive vocation as one of preaching, with its necessary basis in prayer, rather than the diaconal ministry of "waiting on tables."

Some readers of this passage, such as the late Verna Dozier, see in it the beginnings of clerical stratification in the church, but I see it as a necessary ordering. The apostles never suggest that they are too good or too important to wait on tables, but simply that their ministry lies elsewhere. Indeed, the apostles describe their own call to preaching as a ministry of service: they wish to devote themselves to prayer and to "serving [*diaconia*] the word." The deacons, on the other hand, are ordained to serve tables and the people who sit at them. Thus the Twelve serve Christ through preaching the word, while the Seven serve Christ by waiting on his poor.

We ignore the varieties of service in the church at our peril; we cannot exercise our distinctive ministries if we are busy doing somebody else's. Preaching is a fundamental pastoral responsibility, but it requires time for study, for prayer, and for mulling over the texts. Overwork undermines this process. The priest who is trying to do it all—exhausted, overextended, and spiritually depleted—cannot practice the relaxed receptivity to the Word from which good preaching springs. It is our interdependence in the body of Christ that makes the full expression of our common mission possible. When the charisms of the whole body are recognized, trained, and employed, priests can be freed from the false burden of omnicompetence. The Spirit, whose life animates the church, thus liberates us for the proper tasks of our calling, preaching being one of these distinctive ministries.

PREPARING TO PREACH

But how do we begin to preach? If only it could depend on coming up with a workable strategy, the proper technique—maybe reading over the lections a few times, reviewing the commentaries, perhaps taking a look at a journal article or two dealing with our texts, and then coming up with a bright idea, some new angle for this week. But that doesn't work, does it? Inspiration will not appear on demand; the Word of God, as the children in Narnia might say, "is not a tame lion." We cannot grab at the Word and manipulate it for our own ends, not even to get the sermon done in time for Sunday.

Preparing to preach often means finding ourselves up against the wall. There is usually some degree of panic beforehand: Will I have anything to say? Will I bore them? Am I pushing too hard? Have we become too complacent and now need to be challenged? What price will I pay if I say this? Uh oh, so-and-so might really be mad about this one! And finally: Good grief, what can I say about *these* texts? Anyone who preaches regularly can understand why plagiarism occurs among clergy. Ready or not, Sunday comes every seven days.

Fortunately, there are some fine guides to the art of preaching to hone our native talents and put them to their best use. For those whose education prior to seminary did not cultivate literary skills—the competence to read, enjoy, and unpack texts—learning to preach will undoubtedly entail some uphill stretches. I believe that we have a fundamental responsibility to preach from the biblical text, and the meaning of that text is rarely self-evident. Our preaching also needs to take into account its liturgical setting, including the season of the liturgical year or feast day. Good preaching springs from a mix of diverse gifts: a natural aptitude for public speaking, an education that entailed the close reading of texts, a lively and sympathetic imagination, and a passion to communicate the gospel. Even the textbooks on preaching, however, generally agree that there is more to this craft than learning a workable approach to preaching, "finding your voice," or hitting upon the homiletic style that seems to fit your personality, the community, and the occasion. Preaching finally depends on grace, and grace is the wild card in preaching.

The grace of inspiration can sometimes seem in short supply. Knowing that we cannot manufacture it for ourselves may make us edgy and anxious. Some clergy suspect that other preachers may be genuinely inspired, but they, for some reason, are not. So they just press on with the job, maybe looking at the commentaries, hoping for that flash of insight, getting the words down on the page. Since the wild card of grace has not shown up in the hand they have been dealt, they play their best with the cards they have.

But the Dealer has stacked the deck in our favor. Grace is waiting for us. Only we can't queue up for inspiration, demanding our weekly dole. It takes patience, and prayer, and a certain interior environment to receive it. Our posture has to be more like Annie Dillard's as she described taking her post on Tinker Creek, sometimes watching and waiting in silence, at other times actively pursuing the animals she longed to see:

> I can stalk them in either of two ways. The first is not what you think of as true stalking, but it is the *Via negativa,* and as fruitful as actual pursuit. When I stalk this way I take my stand on a bridge and wait, emptied. I put myself in the way of the creature's passage, like spring Eskimos at a seal's breathing hole. Something might come; something might go. I am Newton under the apple tree, Buddha under the bo. Stalking the other way, I forge my own passage seeking the creature. I wander the banks; what I find,

I follow, doggedly, like Eskimos haunting the caribou herds. I am Wilson squinting after the traces of electrons in a cloud chamber; I am Jacob at Peniel wrestling with the angel.[2]

Her two approaches correspond to the two chief forms of seeking God through meditative practice: the negative way and the affirmative way, the passive and the active. She is well aware of how these ascetical precedents inform her own methods, as her references to the Buddha and Jacob show. She even names the *via negativa* for us.

For many Christians, including clergy, "meditation" may seem too lofty and impractical to be a viable preparation for preaching. In our workaday world, with its privileging of the practical and disdain for the "unrealistic," it is easy to ignore the claim regular meditative practice might have on us. Meanwhile, it is we who become unreal, as we drift along on the surface of daily events, bounced from one obligation to the next. Meditation is not a flight from reality, but an encounter with it. When Annie Dillard gives herself over to the contemplation of muskrats, just watching them, without asking anything from the moment except to look at these creatures and drink in the reality before her, she can write of this experience: "I have often noticed that even a few minutes of this self-forgetfulness is tremendously invigorating. I wonder if we do not waste most of our energy just by spending every waking minute saying hello to ourselves."[3]

But how do we cultivate self-forgetfulness? The project seems like a self-contradiction: the more we try, the more we are bound to fail. What moved Dillard to self-forgetfulness was her fascination with the animals she was stalking. Cannot we be similarly delighted by God? Could not God so draw our loving attention that we might actually forget ourselves for a bit?

For preachers, this apophatic awareness forms an indispensable backdrop to our preaching. It can save us from theological hubris—the absurdity of thinking that we could ever have the di-

---

2. Annie Dillard, *Pilgrim at Tinker Creek* (New York: HarperCollins, 1974), 186–87.
3. Dillard, *Pilgrim at Tinker Creek,* 200.

vine mystery all wrapped up. It teaches us humility—even our most sublime language about God will distort and fall short of the divine reality. We will never exhaust the truth about God, for there is always more. "No one has ever seen God," St. John's prologue asserts, and yet in the very next breath, the evangelist makes this stunning affirmation: "It is God the only Son, who is close to the Father's heart, who has made him known" (John 1:18). The revelation of the Incarnate Word is the foundation of the Christian *via affirmativa,* the path to God through the created order, grounded in the Incarnation. Preaching thus oscillates between these two poles. On the one hand, words can never fully capture the divine mystery. Preaching must begin by dwelling in silence, waiting upon God to open the text, to give us a word. On the other hand, God does speak, and the preacher must give witness to that word. Anna Carter Florence says it well: "The preacher tells what she has seen and heard *in the biblical text and in life,* and then confesses what she believes about it."[4]

What we see and hear in the biblical text, though, will depend in part on what we are seeing and hearing in our lives as they unfold in time. When we plunge into the texts, we will not always see and hear what we heard the last time: there may be something quite new awaiting us. All sorts of things have happened to us since the last time we preached on this text, so we have to allow the richness of Scripture to intersect with the various forces in our lives.

When I look back on more than two decades of preaching on familiar texts, I am struck by how my response to many passages has changed over the years. The parable of the Prodigal Son (Luke 15:11–32), probably the best known of Jesus' parables (along with the story of the Good Samaritan), shows up in the Sunday lectionary every three years in the middle of Lent. Its themes of repentance and mercy are appropriate to this penitential season. If your experience is anything like mine, however, your reading of the parable keeps moving; it never seems like quite the same story.

---

4. Anna Carter Florence, *Preaching as Testimony* (Louisville, Ky.: Westminster John Knox Press, 2007), xiii.

For a long time the younger son occupied my attention, the one actor in this complicated story for whom the parable is traditionally named. In other words, he has become the "identified patient" of the family, and it's not hard to see why. This boy has the effrontery to ask for his inheritance during his father's lifetime. Could any child say, "I wish you were dead" more clearly than that? Astonishingly, the father gives him his share and lets him go. Only when the boy has blown all the money and is reduced to envying the pigs their swill does he "come to himself" and decide to return home. But he is not repentant, only looking out for Number One, as usual. Conscience was never this kid's strong suit. He figures he can get a better deal working for his father than for his Gentile master and works up a speech calculated to trigger the necessary parental meltdown.

In my own meditations and preaching on this parable during this time, I tended to focus on the father's warm embrace of this wayward son. He receives him back simply because he came back: the younger son didn't deserve it and wasn't even sorry. On this level the parable seems to dramatize how "Christ died for us while we were yet sinners." Perhaps when the father kills the fatted calf and throws a big homecoming party for him, the boy might at last realize just how deeply he is loved. Maybe by then he will see the grace that had surrounded him since childhood. The parable seemed to invite us not so much to grovel in repentance as to respond, as we hope the younger son finally did, to meet love with love.

After a while, however, my interest shifted to the other brother who, in his own way, also stands in need of redemption. His case is a harder nut to crack. It took me a long time to pay attention to this older sibling because I was so much like him. In fact, I managed to ignore him until I actually started to have dreams about the parable, with myself starring as the elder brother! You see, in my own family of origin, although I am not the eldest, I was certainly always the "good girl." Some of my siblings did not share my aspirations to moral perfection, and I leave your imagination to fill in the gaps in that story. The older brother in the parable, however, needs to be cut some slack from the homiletical beating he usually gets; he was, at least, trying. In his engaging study of the parables of Jesus, William Brosend observes that it is unfair to make the older brother "the poster boy for everything pompously pious in Christian tradition"; and he finds his complaint to his father, "You have never given me even a young goat so that I might celebrate with my friends" a "sadly endearing" detail in the story.[5] I know how easy it is for the "good child" to feel ignored while the parents' emotional energy is spent on the troublemaker. In Jesus' parable we do not know what happened to either brother in the long run; the story remains open-ended. Does the elder brother soften to his father's pleading and join the party? Or does he continue to stand outside and sulk? Is the younger brother moved by this final display of fatherly love or does he continue to sponge off his parents?

Eventually, of course, I came to the father, perhaps the central character in the story. All the action swirls around his relation to each son, and even their relations to each other seem mediated through him. Does he stand for God? Older commentaries and works of Christian art over the centuries see him that way: as the embodiment of divine mercy toward us. Given the context of this parable, one of three stories Jesus told in response to those who were "grumbling and saying, 'This fellow welcomes sinners and eats with them,'" such an interpretation seems justified. But it was my own experience of parenthood that opened the figure of the father for me as never before. Anyone who has a child over the age of ten will know how exquisitely wounding children can be. Some hurts need to be corrected; others passed over in silence; all of them have to be absorbed. Now that my own daughter is a teenager, I find myself thinking over the mystery of freedom the parable dramatizes. The father (and mother, presumably) must relinquish the illusion of control. His anxious waiting for his younger son, and his earnest pleading with his older son, make it clear that the father is very much on the receiving end of the action. There is something divine in his vulnerability, his willingness to let go, this consent to the freedom of the other.

5. William Brosend, *Conversations with Scripture: The Parables* (Harrisburg, Pa.: Morehouse Publishing, 2006), 46.

In telling these parables, Jesus was inviting us to reflect on our own ordinary human experiences to see who we are and who God is. To ask whether the father in the story stands for God or is just an ordinary father misses the point. The father in the parable is, to be sure, an extraordinarily magnanimous man, but I have known other parents who were just as forgiving, patient, and accepting. The parable invites us to burrow into our own circumstances to see how each member of this cast of characters is located within our range of experience. They help us see the currents of grace in which we are already swimming. If the father stands for God, and I think to some extent he does, we understand him best by getting some glimpse into divine love as it is revealed in the stories we are ourselves living.

This does not mean that we have to "tell our story" every time we preach. Sometimes personal narrative is helpful so long as we don't stop there, for the goal of preaching is to open the Scriptures up in such a way that the listeners in the congregation can also find themselves in the text. One way or another, our meditation needs to elicit theirs.

PRAYER, PREACHING, AND SILENCE

Because preaching depends upon grace, we will need to pray in order to preach. Liturgical prayer, while essential, is not sufficient. We need to find ways to pray long enough for our anxiety to move into trust, for our scattered thoughts to give way to listening, and for our desire to manage the situation to hand itself over to God. For this to occur, some measure of deliberate silence in our daily lives is critical. Before we can hear the word of God, we need first to hear what is already buzzing inside us: the drone of our thoughts and obsessions, our fears and aspirations, our regular litany of gripes. Our own thoughts are often not pleasant company, so we manage to steer clear of solitude by keeping our schedules packed. Over time, however, the consequences of habitually avoiding ourselves and God are disastrous for our preaching, pastoral care, and personal lives.

Prayer can begin very simply, but it must be honest as we articulate before God our jumble of concerns, worries, and hopes. By releasing them to the judgment of God, they can begin to get sorted out. We may learn which of our desires, if any, are of the Spirit. Only then might we find ourselves on the edges of that potent silence in which God's Word might be spoken. According to Ignatius of Antioch, the Incarnate Word issues from the fathomless depths of divine silence: the one God "manifested himself through Jesus Christ his Son, who is his Word that came forth from silence."[6] We can participate in that divine silence, and from that sacred ground pray with the scriptural texts. For however else preachers may engage in prayer, they must regularly return to the practice of *lectio divina*. Sitting in meditative openness to the scriptural text seems to me both an essential preparation for channeling the Word and an inexhaustible quarry for preaching itself.

Regular scriptural meditation puts us in that place where the Spirit can "take what is Christ's" and reveal it to us. It brings us into an encounter with Jesus not simply as an historical figure, but as a living presence—the Risen Lord. It can move our sense of Jesus away from fantasy and projection, especially if we allow ourselves to be baffled, surprised, and sometimes undone by the untamed Lion of Judah. In meditation we come to know Christ and we come to know ourselves in a new way. What Rowan Williams observes about the way meditation on Jesus' humanity figured in the spirituality of Teresa of Avila might also be said of meditation on the gospels generally: that it is a matter of "coming to know ourselves *through* Christ." Thinking about our own situation in relation to that of Jesus might strike some Christians as presumptuous or even blasphemous: Who are we to be comparing ourselves to Jesus? However, the point of such meditation is not unvarnished identification with Christ, even if we have allowed our personal circumstances to prompt consideration of parallel

---

6. Ignatius of Antioch, *Epistle to the Magnesians* 8, in *The Apostolic Fathers,* vol. 1, Loeb Library Classics, ed. Bart D. Ehrman (Cambridge, Mass.: Harvard University Press, 2003, 2005), 249.

instances in Jesus' life or ministry. Rather, we reflect on the gospels "to set our feelings in a new context. . . . In other words, Christ as companion both affirms and challenges our emotions. There is significant interplay between identification with Christ and confrontation with Christ."[7]

Lectio divina asks us to read the Bible in a manner other than the way many of us were trained because it makes us read the Scriptures slowly. Since the books of the Bible cover a wide range of historical periods and literary genres, most of our formal education in biblical studies had us read extensively in the Bible, grasp broad concepts, and digest a good deal of detail. That has its value, but the method of *lectio divina* is just the opposite: we read a modest amount of text in order to appropriate it in depth and discover how the Word of God might be speaking to us through the words of Scripture. Early Christian writers spoke of it as a process of rumination, and the bovine associations connected to that word—of cows chewing and rechewing their cud—was deliberate. Medieval monks went on to develop their own teaching about *lectio divina* by observing four successive aspects to it: reading (*lectio*), pondering (*meditatio*), praying (*oratio*), and gazing (*contemplatio*). This scheme is a kind of map, and like most maps it offers a picture of how to get there from here, but it should not be mistaken for the trip itself. In practice, the terrain may feel rather different. Above all, *lectio divina* should not be construed as something complicated or abstruse. It is mostly a matter of reading slowly, of allowing our associations and feelings to surface naturally, and then of praying from whatever stirs in the depths of the heart. *Lectio* sometimes issues in the quiet contemplation to which the monks referred: a simple resting in an insight, grace, or sense of God's presence.

The gospels themselves give us clues about the meditative reading of sacred texts. Early in his gospel, St. Luke presents his readers with a model of faithful discipleship in Mary, the mother of Jesus. Twice in his infancy narrative—once after the visit of the shepherds at Bethlehem, and again after losing and finding the twelve-year-old Jesus in the temple—we are told that Mary "trea-

---

7. Rowan Williams, *Teresa of Avila* (Harrisburg, Pa.: Morehouse Publishing, 1991), 89.

sured all these words and pondered them in her heart" (Luke 2:19; cf. 2:51). Here, at the start of his gospel, Luke seems to want to coach us about how to read his text. He is going to hold Jesus before our eyes, but we are not to view Jesus dispassionately and from a distance. Luke wants to move his readers to faith or, if they are already believers, to a more secure and informed faith. So early on he offers an example in Mary, responding to the baffling events of her child's life by simply taking them in and meditating on their significance. We are to do the same. As the evangelist relates event after event, we are to "treasure all these words and ponder them in our hearts." Such rumination will not make us eyewitnesses of the Lord, of course, any more than Luke himself, but through the meditative pondering of the gospel, we can come to know Jesus.

In all forms of true prayer, including meditative prayer, the Holy Spirit takes the lead. Although it may seem to us that we are taking the initiative when we decide to pray, our desire for prayer is actually a response to the stirrings of the Spirit. Our inclination toward prayer witnesses to God's prior activity and desire for us: "Likewise the Spirit helps us in our weakness; for we do not know how to pray as we ought, but that very Spirit intercedes with sighs too deep for words" (Rom. 8:26). As Martin Smith observes: "In prayer we are never 'getting a conversation going.' We are continuing a conversation which God has begun."[8] We are not alone when we pray, and we do not have to wonder whether God is really listening.

When we take up a scriptural passage for meditation, a many-layered event is in the works. We are responding to some nudge of the Spirit, perhaps experienced as an inner restlessness or spiritual hunger. Perhaps we just need contact with God. By opening the Bible, we are situating ourselves in a stream of tradition that reaches back millennia. While the text may be taking our imagination back through history, something is happening in the present moment that might be described as transhistorical. The Spirit who first inspired the author of the passage we are reading is now

---

8. Martin L. Smith, *The Word is Very Near You: A Guide to Praying with Scripture* (New York: Church Publishing, 1989, 2006), 18. This is an excellent introduction to *lectio divina* and other forms of Christian meditation.

taking hold of the text and declaring it to us, confronting us with its truth, at whatever level that truth can be perceived. The Gospel of John seems to anticipate just this sort of occurrence within the community of believers when Jesus declares to the apostles in his Farewell Discourse, "I still have many things to say to you, but you cannot bear them now. When the Spirit of truth comes, he will guide you into all the truth. . . . He will take what is mine and declare it to you" (John 16:12–14).

Although we exist only within some particular moment in time, the Spirit is not confined by that moment. The words and actions of Jesus, while transacted in the past, have the power to become a living reality: "He will take what is mine and declare it to you." Just as the Holy Spirit is invoked in the eucharist to transform ordinary bread and wine into Christ's Body and Blood, so a kind of *anamnesis* occurs with the reading of Scripture. The Spirit enlivens the ancient text, making us contemporaries with the writers of the words of the Scriptures. The connection here between word and sacrament is not accidental, since scriptural texts were originally written not for private reading but for communal use, usually within the context of worship. New Testament scholar Christopher Bryan notes that the Gospel of Mark, for instance, was probably first proclaimed aloud in the liturgy, as dramatic readings that were emotionally charged performances with plenty of scope for audience reaction and participation. He likens this sort of public reading to the interactive preaching in a traditional African-American congregation of today. The effect on the listeners would be explosive as the past became present: "The audience would feel themselves to be at once hearing what had happened, and yet experiencing it and living in it *now*. They would hear how Jesus addressed their predecessors, and they would hear Jesus addressing *them*. Sometimes they would hear both at once, and sometimes one rather than the other."[9]

Even when we read Scripture privately, we read it within a much larger community. It remains the church's book written for the community of faith to nurture faith. Just as we always pray as

---

9. Christopher Bryan, *The Resurrection of the Messiah,* forthcoming from Oxford University Press.

members of Christ's body, no matter how solitary we are, so in the faithful reading of Scripture we are sharing in a collective event; the community is never far in the background. The church also stands under the word of Scripture, as church reformers have reminded us, in a complex and dynamic relationship. But the communal matrix of the biblical books must never be forgotten. We are indebted to countless believers before us: those who wrote the texts, compiled them, edited them, copied them, printed them, translated them, commented upon them, and preached them before they ever reached us. A lively sense of the vast biblical community to whom we are responsible, and from whom we can draw inspiration and strength, is necessary for preaching. We do not speak on our own behalf, but preach the gospel that has been entrusted to the church.

A number of writers, both teachers of homiletics and teachers of prayer, suggest first approaching a biblical text without resorting to commentaries or other scholarly works to assist our exegesis of the passage before us. There is certainly something to be said for a fresh engagement with a text in order to listen to it with "the ears of the heart." Many texts can speak to us pointedly and profoundly if we simply let the passage say what it seems to want to say. The popularity of African Bible study, a form of small group *lectio divina* in which a biblical passage is read several times over with ample space given for silent reflection, is a tribute to the enduring power of Scripture to address us "where we live."

Seldom, however, do preachers approach a text purely on its own terms; just reading a passage from a well-annotated Bible gives us access to layers of accumulated erudition. Especially if we have preached the round of the lectionary a few times, many of us come back to texts that we have previously studied with the help of commentaries and other guides. Or at least we should have. Sound biblical exegesis can, at the least, deliver us from naïve or erroneous readings and, at best, enormously enrich our understanding. I am not suggesting that we engage in scriptural meditation or take the initial steps toward preparing a sermon buried under piles of commentaries, but it sometimes happens that the work of scholars can open levels of insight for us or dispel a problem. Either possibility might lead to a breakthrough in prayer or in preaching.

If the only time in which we engage in *lectio divina* is when we are called upon to preach, however, it will prove difficult to maintain any purity of intention in our prayer. Instead of approaching the text with openness of mind and heart, discovering in scriptural prayer a renewed spontaneity, we are likely to find ourselves driven by our craving for that coveted brainstorm. But for those who regularly practice scriptural meditation, praying the texts on behalf of the congregation for whom we will preach becomes an extension of pastoral intercession. What might God's word *for them* be? How is God approaching us through this text? How does this passage change or enlarge our sense of God or Jesus? What is the divine perspective at work here? We cannot really know until we approach the text in a posture of receptivity on behalf of our people. As Richard Lischer writes, "The preacher reads texts on behalf of others and *turns* them, so that they might once again release the brilliance of their witness to Jesus Christ. The genius of preaching lies in the discovery of this witness, which occurs amidst prayer, struggle, and exegesis, in a moment of theological insight. In the preacher, the imagination is a theological faculty."[10]

The better our sense of the community, the more we will be attuned to the particular word God might be speaking to them through us. The more heartfelt our love for the congregation, the more sensitive we will be to the Spirit's leading, the more patient in waiting and working until a clear sense of the sermon's direction is given. A long pastorate in one place need not doom us to rehearsing our standard sermon themes year after year. On the contrary, we usually notice the specific ways the paschal mystery is unfolding in our congregation only over the long haul. Parishes never stand still, but change typically takes place slowly. A long pastorate can gradually open our eyes to what is going on: the steadily changing contours of sin and grace, of temptation and blessing. All this gets woven into our preaching.

---

10. Richard Lischer, *A Theology of Preaching: The Dynamism of the Gospel*, rev. ed. (Durham, N.C.: The Labyrinth Press, 1992), "Preface," n.p.

Those of us who serve within traditions that use a lectionary to determine the Scripture readings are relieved of an immense burden. Although we may chafe at times over individual selections, wondering why these verses were included or those were omitted, the genius of the lectionary lies precisely in its power to move us beyond our comfort zone. By exposing us and our congregations to large chunks of Scripture over the course of three years, the lectionary weakens the temptation to use the Bible merely to bolster our pet ideas or to preach on our favorite motifs week after week. Over time, we are more likely to preach something closer to the "whole gospel," not just select portions of it. Since the biblical texts are in many respects in conversation with each other, the lectionary also helps protect us and our congregation from narrow, idiosyncratic readings. Lectionary-based preaching forces us to stand under the Word, to let it search us out, probing us with its penetrating light. In *The Intrusive Word*, William Willimon argues that the task of the evangelical preacher is to bring people before God, not to protect them from God.[11] We cannot protect ourselves, either—in prayer our defenses can start to come down.

Just as administering the sacraments engenders a sense of spiritual poverty, so too sermon preparation requires radical dependence upon God. As we have already observed, the Jesus of John's gospel is stripped of any word of his own devising: all comes from God. This includes the word of preaching and teaching. When Jesus went up to the temple to teach during one celebration of the Festival of Booths, some of his listeners expressed astonishment at the depth and authority of his teaching—a capability they regard as all the more remarkable given Jesus' lack of formal rabbinic training. Jesus takes them aback: "My teaching is not mine but his who sent me" (John 7:16). The statement is two-edged. On the one hand, he speaks in utter humility: "My teaching is not mine." Yet on the other, he claims ultimate authority: "but his who sent me." The word he speaks is none other than God's.

In the previous chapter, we noted how Karl Rahner, among others, makes a comparable claim for the words spoken in sacra-

11. William H. Willimon, *The Intrusive Word: Preaching to the Unbaptized* (Grand Rapids, Mich.: Eerdmans, 1994), 68.

mental rites. "I baptize you," "I absolve you," "This is my Body"—the sacramental formulae catch the priest up in a similar, paradoxical authority. On these occasions the priest is bereft of any pretense to personal power, yet endowed with the full voice of Christ: "By virtue of these words, the priest is completely stripped of power and completely powerful, because they are not his words any more at all, and they are wholly the words of Christ." Not our own words but his who sent us.

While this is also true of preaching, we know that preaching is a more complicated matter. We work more in the dark. Another kind of humility is required. We cannot be timid about God's call to us to preach. "Rekindle the gift of God that is within you through the laying on of my hands," is Paul's counsel to a flagging Timothy, "for God did not give us a spirit of cowardice, but rather a spirit of power and of love and of self-discipline" (2 Tim. 1:6–7). Because grace is given in the laying on of hands, a serious responsibility falls to the ordained to keep the fire ablaze by returning to its source. God will provide those he has called to preach with his Word, but it is not simply infused into us like an intravenous drip. The gift of preaching depends, in part, on our receptivity toward it, our readiness to share in the prayerfulness, trust, and obedience of Christ. It also involves hard work.

WHAT DO WE NEED TO KNOW?

"Be transformed by the renewing of your minds."
(Romans 12:2)

What does the preacher need to know in order to preach? Since we are called to address matters of ultimate significance—God and creation, sin and salvation—continued reading in the theological and spiritual tradition is imperative. It is not that our preaching will consist of academic discourses on these topics. We need to study in order to gain greater clarity *in our own minds* about the ways of God, for only then can we speak about them coherently and persuasively to others. The ability to think clearly about theological issues will shape our reading of the biblical texts and influence the kinds of questions we bring to them.

Since in preaching we are attempting to bring the congregation into a conversation with the Scriptures, our pastoral understanding of the parish will also figure in our preaching. Sermon preparation might become an occasion for serious pastoral reflection on the movements of grace and temptation within the parish as a whole and perhaps in the lives of individual members, although responsible preaching never breaches confidences or exposes the vulnerabilities of particular people. In trying to address both the congregation and each person in it, just about anything that enlarges our sense of the range of human experience will help. Novels and poetry, films and plays, music, current affairs—all contribute to our formation as mature human beings. These are neither homiletical sidelines nor covert strategies for coming up with fetching sermon illustrations, however. It is, rather, a matter of our developing into full human beings, people of wisdom, insight, and compassion, who understand how God in Christ has healed and transfigured the human condition.

While some clergy love to study and crave more opportunities for it, others look for every chance to evade serious, extended thinking. Study and theological reflection were for seminary; now they are engaged in "real ministry." Consider Fred Craddock's description of pastors who

> creep like snails to the study, force themselves in, sit down, line up sheets of paper, sharpen pencils, go for coffee, rearrange the papers, resharpen the pencils, hope the phone rings, cock the ear to hear the bleating of a stray lamb lost somewhere in a dark ravine, and sure enough—! There are a thousand voices, and reasonable ones, too, which argue that the shepherd's place is among the flock. No one can counter that. And, in addition, with the flock is where the satisfactions are, the clear reminders that one is a minister. But not until a minister is persuaded that working in the study *is* being among the flock, and not until the flock ac-

cepts that fact, can a ministry, and especially a preaching ministry, attain full stature and be consistently effective.[12]

The problem is rarely with "the flock," whose gratitude for good preaching is usually boundless. They will not begrudge the pastor time for sermon preparation, whether it consists in the larger engagement with the life of the mind or the more immediate work of study and sermon writing. People do not come to church anymore because social respectability requires an appearance from them, but because they are looking for ways to make sense of their lives:

> The old patter about those who dress up on Sunday to sit in church and play the hypocrite is out of date. The reverse is more true. It is the world that six days a week demands pretension and hypocrisy that has become a burden. These people come on Sunday hopeful of that which is becoming increasingly interesting these days: the truth, shared in a context where the push to impress and be impressed is absent. The fact that they choose to come to the sanctuary rather than elsewhere is clue enough for the preacher that those whose steady diet is cake still have an appetite for bread.[13]

In fact, an appreciative, attentive congregation can consistently draw forth the preacher's best efforts. Just as teaching forces us to come to grips with a subject as never before, so preparing a sermon can activate in us memories, insights, and connections we scarcely knew were there.[14] I can remember as a newly ordained deacon the thrill of having the gospel reading pass right through me— through my body, through my voice—as I was permitted to proclaim the text in the eucharistic liturgy. How much more does the Spirit have to dig deep into long forgotten or only half-conscious memories as we struggle to speak in our own words something of

12. Fred B. Craddock, *Preaching* (Nashville: Abingdon Press, 1985), 72.
13. Fred B. Craddock, *As One Without Authority*, rev. ed. (St. Louis, Mo.: Chalice Press, 2001), 57.
14. Simon Tugwell, OP, *The Way of the Preacher* (Springfield, Ill.: Templegate Publishers, 1979), 76.

God's word. Salvation then comes to us even before it reaches our listeners, as we sense how hidden or buried parts of ourselves are now coming under the reign of God.

It is well known among clergy that when we preach, however much we have taken the congregation into our planning, we preach first of all to ourselves. Conscientious preparation leads us into that holy space where God is likely to act and where we are likely to surrender. A priest once told me that she was moved to preach on a certain text without knowing why, until an unexpected family crisis the very next day revealed the reason: her own words were exactly what she needed to hear. More typically, the words, images, or puzzling parts of Scripture that grab our attention indicate something about our own condition. We gravitate toward those verses because they hold a blessing for us; they are beckoning us to attend to a matter of some consequence. Only we usually have to work with them for a while to know why.

A seasoned preacher once gave me the advice, "Show them how grace works." Grace takes hold of us in the warp and woof of everyday events, and the process often begins with memories of what has transpired in our own flesh, our own histories. Once when I was confronted with the gospel in which Jesus cures a man with a speech impediment (Mark 7:32–37), I was taken back to the time when I first realized that I spoke with a lisp. I was ten years old. I hadn't a clue that I spoke any differently from anyone else until my best friend's father mimicked my speech. Like most mimics, he thought his performance was highly amusing. But I was embarrassed and that, in turn, rendered me tongue-tied and speechless. How could I say anything and not open myself to still more ridicule? Fortunately for me, my teachers noticed around the same time that I had not yet outgrown my childhood lisp. They recommended me to a speech therapist who was engaged by the school. Working with this kind, grandmotherly, and highly capable woman, I learned how to hear and then articulate the sounds that I had previously been confusing.

The odd thing was that I had not thought about this episode for decades. In fact, I don't believe I had ever reflected on it at all. It happened and then was gone—wholly forgotten until I found myself mulling over the situation of the man Jesus cured—a man who was deaf and who spoke with difficulty, if at all. In my case, I had never given thanks for the therapist (no doubt long dead) who had imparted clear speech and renewed self-confidence to me, nor for my teachers and parents who had noticed the problem and addressed it. Preparing the sermon helped me recover this little piece of my past, and as I wove this story into the sermon, the grace of my own small healing so many years ago flooded me with gratitude. The occasion of preaching opened up the meaning of that distant event for me, while opening up the text of the gospel. Perhaps this dim memory rose up because Jesus approached the afflicted man so very tactically, applying his own saliva to the man's tongue and placing his fingers in his ears. As a child, I was initially abashed by the therapist's insistence that I place my hands on her throat and my own, and sometimes in my mouth, so I could learn to feel how sounds were made. But this hands-on approach cured me.

After preaching on this text, I also began to notice a change in myself as I went about my pastoral rounds. When I would visit someone whose speech had been compromised by a stroke, I found a tiny point of identification with the frustration, isolation, and sense of diminishment that went hand-in-hand with this impairment. I discovered new compassion for a friend who stammered whenever he was nervous. My usual impatience with people who take a long time to say what they want to say lessened a bit. It was as if the healing that began when I was ten years old found its fulfillment in middle age. The grace of Christ touched me anew, by stirring up the recollection of how he had worked through others. Time seems to circle back on itself, as living and dead connect again in the graced arena of memory.

Preaching is a form of witnessing to Christ. It is a pointing toward him in which we assume the stance portrayed in medieval and renaissance paintings of John the Baptist. The forerunner of the Lord is typically shown in a posture of gesturing away from himself toward Jesus: "He must increase, but I must decrease" (John 3:30). Whatever we know of Christ, and however we have come to know it, bears on our witness. In the course of our preaching, we will inevitably tell stories about ourselves and our families not for self-disclosure, but because people need to hear how grace works, what happens when God gets inside the amalgam of human life. What we say about ourselves, therefore, has to be strategic, aimed toward our kerygmatic goal: "For we do not proclaim ourselves; we proclaim Jesus Christ as Lord" (2 Cor. 4:5).

Sometimes, let us admit, even after prayer and study there seems to be no fire in our hearts. In those cases we fall back on doing the best we can, acknowledging that the blockage may be due to our spiritual insensitivity. Or perhaps not—only God knows for sure. Still, it might be a question worth exploring, especially if the condition endures for an extended period, because then we may wish to seek some spiritual guidance. In any case, there is scope for grace here, too, since our frailty and limitation, our dullness and lack of inspiration, all have to be offered up to God in detachment and faith. The results of our preaching are likewise outside our control. It sometimes happens that we are rather pleased with a sermon we have composed, only to have it fall flat on delivery. One of the early Dominicans (and the Dominicans are, after all, the Order of Preachers) observed that mothers love even their homeliest progeny; so too, writers are apt to be enamored of their own creations, no matter how defective![15] Yet it frequently happens that we find out weeks, months, or even years later how a sermon of ours that we judged to be mediocre changed someone's life. As O.C. Edwards observes:

> Part of the mystery of preaching is that much of what it accomplishes was never envisioned by the preacher. Anyone who has preached often has had experiences of discovering that what was said in a homily had peculiar appropriateness for someone in the congregation whose presence or need had not been anticipated. And the way people hear things is often not what one intended to convey, but for them it is more important than what was intended. Such "coincidences" happen more often with those who consider

---

15. Tugwell, *Way of the Preacher*, 43.

prayer to be an important part of their preparation for preaching.[16]

The opposite can happen, too. Grace can be rejected, and the truth scorned. Because sin can create indifference, hostility, and hardness of heart, we simply cannot engineer the upshot of our preaching or fret about saving face. We have to be careful about interpreting—or overinterpreting—our pastoral failures. It is easy to lay blame upon either the congregation or ourselves in order to regain a sense of being in charge. Judicious pastoral reflection may be appropriate, but it has to be framed within the mystery of sin and grace, whose movements often elude us and are plainly beyond our ken. Our job is to preach the gospel as God reveals it to us. There are blessings ready to unfold on every side, because whether we are in the process of conceiving the sermon, delivering it, or recovering postpartum, we are in labor with Christ, and he with us.

VULNERABILITY IN PREACHING

"While I held my tongue, my bones withered away."
(Psalm 32:3)

When we preach we are bound to feel pretty exposed. Since we cannot really preach without allowing ourselves, in prayer, to become more and more transparent to God, this undefendedness is apt to show up in our preaching, too. It is not the tidbits of autobiography that crop up in our sermons that provoke the most acute sense of vulnerability. It is uncovering our passion for God, our love for Christ. There is no one way we do this; it is as varied as our sermons. Even if we are not in the habit of wearing our heart on our sleeve, even if we are not trying to draw attention to

---

16. O.C. Edwards, Jr., *Elements of Homiletic: A Method for Preparing to Preach* (New York: Pueblo Publishing, 1982), 23.

ourselves, we cannot be in love without it showing, especially when talking about the beloved. I know of more than one priest who describes preaching as a kind of undressing before the congregation. It can leave us feeling fragile; it is often exhausting. No wonder clergy often need to take a Sunday afternoon nap.

We can avoid giving this costly testimony. There are strategies for hiding out. We can step back from the text and scrutinize it rather than step into the text, letting it probe us. We can entertain. We can give examples whose point is more than a little obscure. We can offer advice. We can lament the ills of the world. We can scold. We can talk about parish programs. We can thunder under the guise of "prophetic" preaching—more often than not fairly predictable moralizing, practiced by liberals and conservatives alike. All these tactics amount to timid preaching that has lost contact with God.

The offense of which preachers are acutely aware is grandiosity, because we dislike it so much when it shows up in others. It is preaching's most obvious sin. Grandiosity is not confidence about preaching, but patent self-reliance. Perhaps those who preach rarely, or only on major occasions, are susceptible to grandiosity in a way that ordinary parish pastors seldom are. Those who struggle with sermons year round know they must rely on a fresh instance of grace every time they preach. There is simply no other way. Yet there are other, subtler, pitfalls.

For example, preaching offers us regular opportunities to notice the disparity between what we preach and how we live. The Epistle to the Hebrews characterizes the word of God as "living and active, sharper than any two-edged sword, piercing until it divides soul from spirit, joints from marrow; it is able to judge the thoughts and intentions of the heart. And before him no creature is hidden, but all are naked and laid bare to the eyes of the one to whom we must render an account" (4:12–13). Preachers are probed and jabbed by this sharp word all the time. It is mighty uncomfortable, especially if members of our family or household, who know our weaknesses like no one else, are sitting in the congregation when we preach. Even if we are spared seeing the truth about ourselves reflected in the eyes of our nearest and dearest, we still have to look at ourselves in the mirror. What happens over time to the preacher who feels he is a fraud? Who does not practice what she preaches? The constant reminder of this gap between who we are and who we should be can slowly lead a preacher to despair.

Despair can take many forms short of abandoning the faith, the ministry, or those particular communities who know us too well. Instead, we can banish this painful self-knowledge to the edges of our consciousness and carry on. The price we pay for denial, however, is high. It takes considerable effort to maintain a favorable self-image, and even more to keep presenting it to the public. Our actual feelings may begin to elude us as we continue sealing off unsettling insights from our awareness. We engage in pastoral work on autopilot, our prayer becomes perfunctory, and our encounter with Scripture superficial. Since preaching tends to be the barometer of our inner state, all we can do is grind out the required performance each week—theatrical, disconnected, dull, sentimental, avuncular, or whatever fits our persona.

Some clergy cannot bear the tension between their private and public selves and decide to make an end of the hypocrisy. They embarrass their congregations by talking publicly of their ongoing interior struggles or feelings of inadequacy, or resort to crude or vulgar language to show that they, too, have their rough edges. In effect, they turn the tables on their flock, forcing them to worry about the pastor. People then hesitate to come to the priest with a genuine difficulty because they fear that he is too fragile or that her life is a mess.

It is not at all surprising that the encounter with the sharp word of God within our larger ministry of the word provokes in us a need to articulate our unworthiness. Contact with holy things can, or at least should, have the same effect on us. Isaiah's seraphic vision while in attendance at the temple of Jerusalem elicits not pleasure, but anguish: "Woe is me! I am lost, for I am a man of unclean lips, and I live among a people of unclean lips; yet my eyes have seen the King, the LORD of hosts!" (Isaiah 6:5). The prophet is driven to speak of his "unclean lips"—a mouth unfit to announce the Lord's word. It is telling that this passage is one of the lessons prescribed for the ordination of a priest, since Isaiah's dilemma is one all preachers face. We must confront and confess our unworthiness, but we are not left alone to manage by ourselves. Help is at hand, but the remedy is painful. A seraph touches his lips with a live coal, and absolution is pronounced: "Now that this has touched your lips, your guilt has departed and your sin is blotted out" (Isaiah 6:7). The story concludes with the prophet's commissioning: "Here I am: send me!"

A wise priest and friend of mine once said, "Preaching is what comes after we're forgiven."[17] Although priests frequently pronounce absolution for others, at least in the liturgy following the confession of sin, we need to hear it directly for ourselves. We cannot be left out. The Reconciliation of a Penitent is a powerful means of grace for those who bear the burden of pastoral leadership. There exists, in particular, a strong if subtle connection between our vocation to preach and our need for sacramental confession. If we are going to speak God's word without shame, don't we need first to say aloud and in our own words how specifically we have fallen short? We will always feel the hypocrite until we find that arena of freedom where we can speak the truth about ourselves by confessing our sins. Rather than jeopardize our pastoral responsibility toward our flock with indiscreet self-disclosures, in confession we can "open our grief" before God and the church, represented in our confessor. We have to be stripped clean by the Word, and then assured by the most palpable means available to us, a personal absolution, that we really do live by grace and not by our own merits. And we need this experience of release not once, not occasionally, but often. Only then will we feel free enough to preach with both humility and boldness, confident of the grace and mercy of Christ.

The grace of reconciliation carries into other spheres of ministry as well. Consider how our faults are inevitably on display; we make our share of mistakes. The point is not to be so rid of personal frailty that we find ourselves above criticism. On the con-

---

17. Edward C. Coolidge, in an unpublished retreat address, "Jesus' Ministry to Us in Our Preaching," given to the clergy of the Episcopal Diocese of Chicago in February 1991.

trary, we should expect to be regularly practicing reconciliation. Why can't we be wrong and admit it? To have slighted someone and apologize? A young rector once remarked to me, "Being a priest means saying you're sorry a lot." While business and government put a spin on their blunders, admitting only that "mistakes may have been made," in the church we can show confidence in God's mercy by the simple exchange of forgiveness among ourselves.

Preaching is about transformation—of the preacher and of the congregation. The liturgy that is preaching's natural home suggests this. Through the eucharistic liturgy we always being formed and reformed into the body of Christ. It is the task of preaching to break open the scriptural texts that have been read in the Liturgy of the Word, to deepen the congregation's conversion to Christ, to contribute to their formation as the people of God, and to prepare them, in most cases, for Holy Communion. The entire movement of worship is toward transformation into Christ, toward union with him and one another. "Be transformed by the renewal of your minds," counsels St. Paul. Preaching tries to do just that. Like the teaching ministry that is its close analogue, it prepares us to love God with all our mind, as well as with all our heart and strength.

CHAPTER FOUR

SHEPHERDING THE FLOCK

Pastoral Care in the Congregation

"The good shepherd lays down his life for the sheep."
(John 10:11)

PASTOR: THE LATIN WORD for "shepherd." In some churches, "pastor" is the customary form of clerical address— "Pastor Smith" or "Pastor Anne"—while in others, such as the Roman Catholic Church, it is a way of designating the office of the priest in charge of a parish. In the Episcopal Church the bishop is named "chief pastor" of the diocese, and those about to be ordained to the office of presbyter are reminded that they are now called to work as "pastor, priest, and teacher." To be a bishop or priest or pastor is thus to be a shepherd. It may, however, be the most misunderstood facet of our calling. Rather than suggesting a vocation to oversight or *episkope,* "pastoral" has come to be associated almost exclusively with pastoral care, primarily to individuals. The larger dimensions of oversight, including administration, are sidelined, even though these responsibilities point to the heart of the pastoral vocation. Administration has been reduced to obligatory but bothersome management, the work of "running a church." Yet a more expansive and stimulating vision of what it means to be "pastoral" emerges from reflection on the biblical metaphor of shepherding.

The scriptural roots of the shepherding metaphor are deep. In an agricultural society, in which the raising of cattle, sheep, and goats was a significant source of economic livelihood and cultural lore, the God of Israel was perceived as the great shepherd of his people. The opening verse of Psalm 80 begins: "Hear, O Shepherd of Israel, leading Joseph like a flock," and at a time when the pastoral office is in danger of becoming reduced merely to caregiving, it is bracing to realize that the original shepherd of the people of Israel was God. The figure was also used to denote kingship, thus reinforcing its significance as an image of governance. For the prophets of Israel, furthermore, the appearance of the ideal shepherd would be a sign of the messianic age. In Jeremiah's oracles God castigates the false and self-serving shepherds of Israel— her kings—and promises to gather the flock together, a flock disheartened and scattered by exile (Jer. 23:1–5).

It was therefore a bold and even dangerous step for Jesus to speak of himself as a "shepherd" because it could have been interpreted as a claim to the Davidic throne, a political move to position himself as king. But no sooner does Jesus appropriate this messianic role for himself than he reconfigures it, so that in Mark's gospel Jesus predicts his imminent desertion by the disciples by alluding to Zechariah's portrayal of a messianic shepherd-king stricken for his people: "I will strike the shepherd, and the sheep will be scattered" (Mark 14:27; cf. Zech. 13:7). In John's gospel, moreover, the good shepherd will "lay down his life for the sheep." Whatever else "pastoral" might mean, then, it is a calling that must keep the paschal mystery well in the foreground.

St. John's gospel presses the shepherd image in another direction by elaborating themes of intimate mutual knowledge between shepherd and sheep: the shepherd knows the sheep, calls them by their particular names, and keeps them away from destruction. The sheep, in turn, recognize the shepherd's voice, follow his lead, and find true pasture and even eternal life with him. John's richly evocative portrayal of the relationship between Christ and his flock is situated theologically within the even more profound relationship between the Son and the Father: "I am the good shepherd. I know my own and my own know me, just as the Father knows me and I know the Father" (John 10:14–15).

~ἓ℞ἓ~

TENDING THE WHOLE CONGREGATION

"He calls his own sheep by name and leads them out."
(John 10:3)

In popular piety the good shepherd is a figure of gentle, solicitous care, and from early in the church's history this image clearly resonated with Christian experience. One of the first visual representations of Christ, dating to around 250 and found in the catacombs of Rome, portrays Jesus as the good shepherd carrying a sheep upon his shoulders. The parable of the Lost Sheep in both Matthew and Luke helped shape the cluster of associations that attribute an overriding concern for the least and the strayed to the good shepherd—a manifestation of divine compassion embodied in Jesus' own ministry.

The real danger in the popular understanding of the good shepherd, especially for pastors, is to lose sight of the flock as a whole. While it is true that the faithful shepherd leaves the ninety-nine sheep to search for the one that is lost, the force of the parable turns on the assumption that this is an *exceptional* case. Most shepherds are busy watching over the entire flock. Since sheep, unlike birds, do not naturally "flock together," maintaining the unity and integrity of the flock will be a demanding occupation.

Hence the attention we give the wayward, distressed, and troubled members of our churches must take place within our larger pastoral oversight of the flock of Christ. It provides the theological and sacramental context for the care we offer to individuals. Problems arise when the appealing closeness between Christ and each little sheep becomes our sole model for the pastoral vocation. We end up adopting a version of pietism to define our calling.

When pastors come under the spell of pietism in their pastoral practice, they are prone to denigrate or neglect the hard work of oversight in favor of more emotionally satisfying one-to-one pastoral care. Because individualism is already pervasive in American culture, we are apt to slip into this distorted version of "pastoral care" without even noticing. How often clergy are prone to say, "I don't want to get bogged down in administration. I just want to be a pastor." How often bishops are praised when they leave their desks and committee meetings to "be a pastor" to an ailing colleague. Yet the work of administration, when conscientiously engaged, is a truly pastoral vocation of careful, wise, judicious oversight and a gift of the Holy Spirit.

Oversight—*episkope*—is precisely what the shepherd does. The connection between the ministry of the good shepherd and the ministry of pastoral office was already being forged in the writings of the New Testament. First Peter hints as much when it refers to Christ as the "shepherd and bishop of your souls" (1 Pet. 2:25, KJV). While the precise forms of ministerial office were still in flux during this period, it is nevertheless telling that "shepherd" is here linked with *episkopos*—variously translated as "bishop," "guardian," or "supervisor." Oversight means, literally, "seeing over," scanning the wider horizons, looking beyond the immediate; it involves getting and maintaining the big picture.

For the church to retain this broad perspective, her pastors are entrusted with *holding the story* for the sake of the community— a story that is rooted in the past but extends into the scarcely imagined future. Pastors keep the eschatological horizon before the church, since the liturgy, sacraments, and hope toward which we move are all aspects of the new life inaugurated by the resurrection of Christ. Such is the environment in which pastoral oversight is exercised. Hence we see that in the Acts of the Apostles, the capacity to be "a witness with us to his resurrection" was the essential criterion for eligibility in rounding out the vacancy among the Twelve, and it led to the selection of Matthias (Acts 1:15–26). Similarly, in the ordinal of the *Book of Common Prayer*, the very first charge to the bishop-elect is "to be one with the apostles in proclaiming Christ's resurrection and interpreting the Gospel, and to testify to Christ's sovereignty as Lord of lords and King of kings" (BCP 517). The resurrection is key to everything else, and the eschatological note of the charge is unmistakable. That is the story bishops, and all other pastors with them, hold for the community: the gift of God in Christ and the Spirit. If we ourselves live in the daily awareness of the presence of the kingdom, catching glimpses of it here and there while still yearning for its final consummation, we cannot help but bring this sense of holy presence to the meetings we chair or the people we visit.

Since the vocation of pastor is a participation in the ministry of the Good Shepherd, it is another way of describing everything we do as presbyters or bishops. Andrew Purves argues that pastoral care is not a "third" area of responsibility, along with word and sacrament, but the ground of all our responsibilities.[1] Thus we exercise our pastoral vocation when we celebrate and administer the sacraments and when we preach. Indeed, these characteristically priestly responsibilities are entrusted to us at ordination precisely because we are ordained to be pastors, sharing with the bishop in her oversight of the diocese. "To take your share in the councils of the Church," as the presbyter is charged at ordination (BCP 531), does not simply designate the canonical privilege of voting at conventions and synods; this charge specifies an aspect of oversight woven into the fabric of our calling. Sacramental presidency and the authority to preach are fundamentally tied to this deeper vocation of pastoral oversight, and we sense a loss of integrity when the relationship between them is weak or tenuous.

I was jolted into an awareness of the connection between eucharistic presidency and pastoral oversight when, after serving for three years as a Sunday celebrant and preacher for a consortium of parishes, the senior warden in one of them introduced me as their "sacramentalist." This minimalist description, suggesting that I merely dropped in to confect the sacrament for them, surprised me. Later reflection gave me some inkling of how my ministry had come to be perceived in this way. It sprang in part from my role as a regular supply priest, in rotation with other clergy serv-

---

1. Andrew Purves, *Reconstructing Pastoral Theology: A Christological Foundation* (Louisville, Ky.: Westminster John Knox Press, 2004), xxiii.

ing the same group of parishes; it also had some basis in a skewed appreciation of lay ministry. The idea seemed to be that the laity carried on the day-to-day ministry of the church, while I provided the sacramental magic on Sundays. I felt the disconnect—in the parishioners' minds and in my own—between the sacramental and preaching ministry I had been exercising and any real sense of pastoral oversight and care, which was the responsibility of other clergy in the group. I also began to understand why some of the parishes in the consortium repeatedly voiced their desire to have a stable pastoral presence—"their own priest," as they put it. At the level of intuition if not theology, they sensed that the priest needed to be their "parson"—their "person"—the one who sacramentally embodied Christ for them in all facets of pastoral ministry.

In Episcopal polity, the bishop must license a presbyter to engage in the ministry of word and sacrament. Yet there is a certain authority for ministry that also comes over time, as I discovered, from the parish congregation itself. The supply priest or pastor, no matter how gifted, rarely elicits this trust. When we serve as a visiting preacher or celebrant, the authority of ordination is typically respected, and sometimes our ministrations are even received with enthusiasm. Although we are sharing on these occasions in the pastoral oversight of the bishop or local pastor, we usually feel a firmer, more integrated sense of vocation when distinctly priestly ministries are grounded in the regular pastoral oversight of a given congregation. This is not surprising, really. The Good Shepherd knows his own and they know him. The pastoral office can bear most fruit when circumstances allow us really to know the flock and thus share in this dimension of good shepherding.

So whether we are preparing a sermon, visiting the nursing home, meeting with lay leaders to brainstorm a new initiative, teaching a class on Mark's gospel, chairing the vestry meeting, or praying with a troubled adolescent, we are engaged in pastoral ministry. Just as the bishop has a special ministry of unity in the diocese and church universal, so the presbyter becomes a focal point of unity for the parish, as the people find personified in him *their own unity* in Christ. Austin Farrer spoke of the priest this way: "The man who bears the Sacrament is sacramental himself; he is, one might almost say, himself a walking sacrament. He is the appointed flag for Christ's people to rally around: the center of unity to which we hold in every place."[2] The image of a walking sacrament also illuminates the expectation most people entertain of finding evidence of holiness in their priest—the baptismal holiness to which they are themselves called.

After decades of vocational confusion, clergy may believe they have finally hit on what they are supposed to be—a leader, as opposed to a pastoral counselor, manager, change agent, or servant. Scholar George Sumner perceptively notes that many of the key ideas and strategies of the leadership literature are actually part of the church's own patrimony that we are now receiving back secondhand. Just as Twelve Step programs drew much of their inspiration and specific practices from the ascetical literature of the church, so with the literature of leadership:

> It would prove more truly fruitful if it were replanted in the richer spiritual and theological soil from which it came. "Vision," "mission," "culture," "virtues": the key terms are strangely abstract and formal, and they leave the pastor with the task of figuring out what the vision is to be, what sort of culture ought to be inculcated. This is just what we would expect in a do-it-yourself, voluntarist society which has spawned the confusion about the pastoral role in the first place.... The categories of the leadership literature are helpful, and pastors mired in the minutiae of stressful lives would do well to organize their efforts around them. But the content of the vision does not require invention, nor does it benefit from reinvention every time the rectorship changes hands. The vision is provided by close attention to Scripture, read in the light of the Creeds. The mission is to let your lights so shine, to celebrate the sacraments, to practice spiritual disciplines.[3]

2. Austin Farrer, "Walking Sacraments," in *The Truth-Seeking Heart: Austin Farrer and His Writings,* ed. Ann Loades and Robert MacSwain (Norwich: Canterbury Press, 2006), 140.
3. George R. Sumner, *Being Salt: A Theology of an Ordered Church* (Eugene, Ore.: Cascade Books, 2007), 90–91.

An example of the do-it-yourself approach of which Sumner speaks may be found in the widespread trend for each congregation to fashion a parish mission statement for itself. While parishes do need to give regular, focused attention to the distinct contours of mission in their locale, large amounts of time can be wasted drawing up these mission or vision statements that then seem to take on the immutability of holy writ. Most of these labor-intensive statements tend toward the banal and self-congratulatory—"St. Jude's seeks to be a welcoming congregation"—in their effort to express the "uniqueness" of each community. Faith communities are particular, but they are not unique; as Sumner points out, the vision is already provided, and our problem is seeing it. Parish congregations share a faith and theological tradition in common with other Christians. What we need to do, then, is something both more modest and more demanding: to teach and to engage the great tradition of the church and then ponder how to live that faith in our own circumstances. Parish mission statements proliferate when parishes fail to understand that their mission is the same basic mission that they share with the rest of the church: "to restore all people to unity with God and each other in Christ" (BCP 855). This is a profound spiritual calling, but the multiplication of facile mission statements obscures it.

BENEDICTINE MODELS OF LEADERSHIP

We have other models of pastoral leadership now coming to the fore. Over the last few decades, many non-monastic Christians have been drawing inspiration from the *Rule of St. Benedict,* especially as interpreted by Esther de Waal and Joan Chittister, among others. Now pastors are starting to take another step in the reappropriation of this heritage: they are beginning to ponder the role of the abbot in the Benedictine community, the most fully delineated office in the *Rule.* At the beginning of his term as Presiding Bishop of the Episcopal Church, Frank Griswold indicated that he took the Benedictine abbot as his model for episcopacy. It is not hard to see why. Like the bishop, the abbot or abbess carries the shepherd's staff, signifying pastoral authority. The Benedictine abbot is supposed to lead and govern his community, but Benedict insists that he wield his authority moderately, always seeking the counsel of his brothers. Because the authority exercised by Benedictine abbots and abbesses grew out of the charismatic authority of the abbas and ammas of the desert tradition, we see in the *Rule* the ideal blending together of the charismatic authority of personal holiness with the stable authority of ecclesiastical office.

Because abbots and abbesses exercise their ministry for the sake of the community, they must take that community into account whenever they are faced with decisions, both great and small. Taking counsel is so important to community life that Benedict devotes an entire chapter to the subject. Even though the abbot is modeled in many ways on the traditional *paterfamilias* of Roman antiquity, Benedict tempers the abbot's absolute authority in a number of significant ways. For one thing, he repeatedly holds the pattern of Christ before the abbot as his true exemplar. And he is to exercise authority both collegially and communally, by seeking the advice of his brothers, for another:

> As often as anything important is to be done in the monastery, the abbot shall call the whole community together and himself explain what the business is; and after hearing the advice of the brothers, let him ponder it and follow what he judges the wiser course. The reason we have said all should be called for counsel is that the Lord often reveals what is better to the younger. . . . If less important business of the monastery is to be transacted, he shall take counsel with the seniors only, as it is written: *Do everything with counsel and you will not be sorry afterward* (Sir. 32:24).[4]

The Benedictine monastery is not a democracy, but Benedict is aware that the abbot may not possess all available wisdom, even if he does bear final authority for decision-making. Benedict departs

---

4. *The Rule of St. Benedict: In Latin and English with Notes,* ed. Timothy Fry, OSB, *et al.* (Collegeville, Minn.: The Liturgical Press, 1981), 3:1–3, 12–13.

from earlier monastic rules by underscoring the possibility that the divine will might be revealed through an easily overlooked source: the youngest, or newest, members (*iuniori*) of the community. As one Benedictine commentary notes, "On the part of both monks and abbot, this process demands, not political techniques designed to ensure the acceptance of one's own view, but a genuine humility and self-effacement, and an opening of one's mind and heart to the mysterious action of God."[5]

Pastoral oversight is an enormous responsibility. To help ease this burden and to enhance our good judgment, the church calls us to work in concert with others and to seek advice, much as Benedict required of his abbots. Pastors take counsel with each other collegially, sometimes in clergy gatherings, sometimes over lunch, often by telephone or email to seek one another's advice or perspective. We also take counsel with members of our congregations in a variety of settings: staff meetings, conversations with lay leaders, committee and vestry meetings, and gatherings of the entire parish.

Seeking counsel is an exercise in discernment. It comes into play when the best way forward is far from clear. It is not a matter of manipulating people to keep up an appearance of democracy. From the time of the desert ascetics, spiritual writers have taught that authentic discernment requires certain interior dispositions: the desire to do God's will, above all, evidenced outwardly by openness of heart and characterized inwardly by spiritual freedom. If we are captive to particular outcomes, we will render ourselves incapable of true discernment. Listening is fundamental, and we cannot listen when we are itching to advance our point of view, or our minds are racing, or we already know what we want to happen. We can only listen when we believe that God might be speaking to us, however haltingly, through another.

The Benedictine style of leadership seeks consensus through a commonly held vision of the Christian life. Consensus can take a long time to achieve, but it is often worth the wait. Many issues in parishes are highly charged because people are strongly invested in the symbols of religion that are dear to them. If we wish to pre-

---

5. Fry, *et al.*, eds., *Rule of St. Benedict*, 179.

serve and even to enhance the unity of the parish, we have to find ways to move forward together. In these deliberations, it is crucial that every voice be heard and somehow accommodated. In my last parish, the wise stewardship of our historic buildings became an area in which I learned how vital it is to work slowly toward a kind of Benedictine consensus.

Shortly after I arrived, I ventured to raise the question of whether we could consider removing the coverings from our windows. The small stone church, built in 1833, had been constructed with three large, clear glass, arched Gothic revival windows running down both sides of the nave. Two more beautiful windows in the narthex faced the street. However, at the time of the fuel crisis of 1973, three-quarters of each window had been covered in gray insulation to save heat. Only a small rectangle at the bottom of each window, made of the charming, irregular glass produced in the previous century, was unobstructed. The interior of the church, originally designed to be filled with light, was now dim and musty, even on sunny days.

Everyone agreed that it would be wonderful to have the coverings come off, but such a project would, alas, be prohibitively expensive. No one thought that we should simply return the windows to their pre-1973 state because then the heat loss would be substantial. We wanted to be sound stewards of our energy use; it would be irresponsible to waste so much fuel. The only way to let light shine in while still saving heat would be to have each window fitted with custom-made glass insulation. The arches and distinct dimensions crafted by the nineteenth-century architects made this the only viable solution, but as this seemed beyond our small parish's financial reach, we remained in the dark for some time without going forward.

About this time a friend of mine, a nun schooled in Benedictine wisdom, urged me to be patient. An idea had been planted in the community; give it time, she counseled, to germinate and grow. The abbot, she reminded me, offers the vision. Let the community decide whether it will be theirs or not. So I offered the vision, and waited.

For about five years, people would mention from time to time how nice it would be to restore the windows—always followed by, "Too bad we can't afford it." After about eight years, members of the property committee suggested, "Well, why don't we get some new estimates of the cost?" They consulted a specialist in antique window restoration, but the project was still awfully expensive. As more and more people looked at the drawings and weighed the price, however, something quietly changed. They were drawn to the sheer beauty of it. The prospect of having all that light return to the church filled them with joy. One by one, individuals and groups made pledges to cover the cost of restoring the windows; my husband and I sponsored one window in thanksgiving for our ten years in the parish. Finally we had enough funds to begin, and after the work was completed, it turned out the energy retention was even better than in the days of insulation, and during the daylight hours, solar heat poured into the church.

The day the bishop came to rededicate our windows, the church was filled with light and warmth, only some of it coming from outside. People spoke openly about the "light of Christ" and their desire to invite others to share in the "light of the gospel." The restoration of the windows began a new phase in the parish's life characterized by profound thanksgiving for what we had inherited from our forebears combined with a renewed, joyful hospitality toward the larger community in which we were located. A strong sense of the past is inescapable in a New England village, but the parish did not conceive of the church as a museum. It was rather a living legacy—a tradition in the root sense of something to be passed on—that invigorated our common life. The light didn't just come in; it drew us out, too. To our surprise, the opening of the windows opened our hearts more widely to those outside the church, to draw them in, if possible, to share our graced bounty.

~~e9~~

ADMINISTRATION AS PASTORAL CARE

Even a casual reader of the *Rule* will notice how much of it is occupied with the everyday ordering of community life: the pattern of psalmody for various seasons of the year, the distribution of clothing, the serving of meals, the hours for working and sleeping, when to change the towels, what to do when something is broken. It is plain that the monastery offers no escape from the details of administration, especially not for the abbot. For every parish pastor, day-to-day administration and decision-making will loom large, and often we resent this work and chafe under it, feeling overwhelmed by detail. Our vision is foreshortened and our spirits slowly eroded by matters clamoring for attention that do not interest us at all. Some clergy take the route of neglecting administration—parish record keeping, correspondence, scheduling the vestry retreat—preferring to spend their time in what they consider "real" pastoral work: counseling couples, visiting the sick, or representing the church on town committees.

Yet simply consulting our preferences about how we would like to spend our time will not do, for churches, like Benedict's community and ordinary human families, require good order and someone to manage a host of humdrum chores. When they are performed well and carried out with care and love, they foster an environment in which the serious and joyful work of developing human relationships can take place. When thoughtfully executed, parish administration supplies the harmony, efficiency, and beauty in which the defining ministries of the church can then occur. The church exists in the world as an extension of the Incarnation, and her incarnate life will manifest itself not only in the bread and wine of the parish eucharist, but also in the furniture of the parish nursery, or the heating and ventilation system. Parish administration, like managing the economy of the home, is servant ministry, but so is everything else. As Louis B. Weeks observes:

Congregations that effectively handle administrative work often have a transformed understanding of it. They don't do administration *instead* of pastoral care; they engage in church administration *as* pastoral care. They consider good organization requisite for effective mission and evangelism. They understand that most people become more generous when they see time, talents and money efficiently used.... How meetings are run, how new leaders are apprenticed, how the books are kept, how communication is structured, how events and programs are implemented and evaluated—all this is crucial to congregational life, but rarely understood as ministry.[6]

Moreover, these mundane tasks require a certain kind of reflective skill to perceive how grace might be operating in them; pastors need to cultivate their capacity to *see*. What can help? Slowing down, for one thing, and giving the eyes of the heart time to refocus. The prayer and meditation so foundational to preaching turn out to be essential for pastoral oversight as well.

Sometimes we even get an inkling of just how the more prosaic tasks of administrative oversight matter. Once I heard from a man on the other side of the country whose great-grandparents had been married in our parish church sometime in the mid-nineteenth century. Would we check for him? Fortunately, the rector of the church in the 1870s kept careful records, and we were able to provide the full names of this man's ancestors, the date of their marriage, and even the name of the officiating priest. We gave him the information he sought, but he gave us something equally precious: a sense of connection to our own parish history, a fresh appreciation for the communion of saints. All because somebody took a few minutes in 1872 to keep good records.

Finally, deep dissatisfaction with administration may be telling us something we need to hear. Micro-management and perfectionism can lead quickly to feeling overwhelmed. What is keeping us from entrusting some responsibilities to others, handing over

---

6. Louis B. Weeks, "God Is in the Details: Administration as Ministry," in *The Christian Century* 126:2 (January 27, 2009): 10.

real authority for decision-making? From voicing our need for adequate support staff? When we cannot delegate tasks to people of proven reliability or if we constantly redo their work, we exhibit a damaging lack of trust and respect. If we sense we are wasting time in committee meetings, we are probably not alone in our frustration. Boredom is not a gift of the Holy Spirit, but it can be revelatory for us, signaling that something basic has gone awry. If our work together on committees does not entail grappling with some aspect of the mission of the church, then it is working against it. In ascetical terms, it has become a "distraction." It is not uncommon for clergy to be unwittingly in league with each other or their parishioners to so fill up their schedules with churchy busywork that they manage to avoid what matters most: God, prayer, silence, study, and attending to relationships. Infidelity to our vocation can be very subtle, and as religious people we naturally find religious pretexts for it.

PARENTING THE PARISH

"Indeed, in Christ Jesus I became your father through the gospel."
(1 Corinthians 4:15)

Being a faithful pastor is much like being a good parent. It takes wisdom, patience, calmness under pressure, and a sense of the long-term goal. It can overlook the small stuff that can be so distracting and irritating if we let it dominate us. "Disciplined calmness" is how Christopher Bryan describes this virtue of leadership, which partakes "*both* of gentleness *and* of a firmness that remains polite—a calm, disciplined strength. Such strength can exercise clemency and even rebuke with courtesy, precisely because it is the mark of those who know who they are and whose they are."[7]

---

7. Christopher Bryan, *And God Spoke: The Authority of the Bible for the Church Today* (Cambridge, Mass.: Cowley Publications, 2002), 126–27.

Hope is the ground of this patience, and it is essential to both parenting and the pastoral oversight of congregations and individuals. Unlike optimism, which can quickly turn to cynicism when we are faced with disappointment, the virtue of hope looks at the world as it is, full of sin, suffering, and tending toward death. Yet hope sees beyond these things to perceive the world redeemed by Christ. Informed by this vision, hope can afford to be patient. It does not try to force growth prematurely but is watchful for small signs of movement. It refuses to demand, even inwardly, a degree of development not really possible at present because it is confident that God will bring all things to fulfillment in due course. Hope knows how to encourage even baby steps toward maturity in Christ.

To be an elder in the church—that is, a spiritual father or a spiritual mother—is to be directly involved in the vitally creative labor, as "stewards of God's mysteries" (1 Cor. 4:1), of passing on the "faith that was once for all entrusted to the saints" (Jude 3). We are representing not just our local congregation, but also the church through the ages. Much of the power of the "ministry of presence" comes from just that perception. Like it or not, we carry the accumulated weight of church history with us. We pass on a tradition with which we are ourselves viscerally engaged, that is already part of the fabric of our being. Like parents who simply love reading or opera or sailing, we pass on our passion for Christ, the sacraments, the Scriptures, and the saints. We try to transmit a vision of the kingdom of God and invite others, in the name of God, to join in. This is vigorous work. But sharing what we love is also vitally generative.

Generativity of this sort draws upon strong tides of parental energy residing in each of us. It will help if we are aware of these feelings and give thanks for them, so our propensity toward spiritual motherhood or fatherhood does not misfire but rather finds appropriate, creative ends. St. Paul evidently identified both fatherly and motherly passions in himself. To the Corinthians he claimed to have become their "father through the gospel" (1 Cor. 4:15). To the Galatians he lamented, "My little children, for whom I am again in the pain of childbirth until Christ is formed in you" (Gal. 4:19). Some clergy, however, are wary of parental metaphors. Some will charge that using "Father" or "Mother" as a title of address automatically infantilizes the laity. Yet thinking of ourselves as spiritual fathers and mothers need not tend in that direction. After all, adults have parents, too, and we never really outgrow our need for mentoring. Elsewhere I have urged continuing—and in the case of women, adopting—these titles in churches that have traditionally used them.[8] They help locate clergy within a tradition that has recognized the charismatic leadership of both women and men since the desert fathers and mothers of the early church. And these titles help situate clerical authority within the mutual affection and accountability of the eschatological family of Christ.

Those who fear that calling priests by parental titles encourages psychological transference might consider that some such reaction is bound to occur, anyhow. Clergy, no matter what they are called or how they dress, are highly symbolic persons, and transference comes with the territory. However, since we are not functioning in our congregations as therapists (even if we have had such specialized training), we are not in the business of trying to manipulate these psychological force fields one way or another. We just let them be. So long as clergy sit lightly on projections when they come, and are sufficiently self-aware that they do not engage in counter-transference, these submerged but powerful dynamics can result in the healing of memories and relationships for people. When positive transference has done its job, it then recedes. It is apt to diminish in any case, as people come to know us in our specific humanity and less as a mere symbol.

---

8. Julia Gatta and Eleanor McLaughlin, "What Do You Call a Woman Priest?" in *Episcopal Times* (October 1981): 4. See also my article, "The Catholic Feminism of Holy Mother Church," in *St. Luke's Journal of Theology (Sewanee Theological Review)* 29:1 (December 1985): 9–23.

STANDING AT THE FOOT OF THE CROSS

"I know my own and my own know me." (John 10:14)

To exercise oversight in our communities, we will have to know our parishioners well. Gaining this knowledge takes a long time, and we never really come to the end of it; every congregation has a history, and so does each of its members. Pastoral visits to people in their homes will include prayer, sacramental ministrations such as house blessings or home eucharists, and above all conversation about a whole range of topics, including God and the church. Small talk will help establish the relationship at the outset, so attentive listening is crucial. Our parishioners' sense of their place in the church and how they understand God are frequently hidden just beneath the surface of the conversation. As pastoral theologian Thomas Oden observes:

> If the pastor is not equipped to recognize where profoundly religious assumptions are lodging quietly in seemingly worldly concerns, the pastor has not thought enough theologically about the body, the family, politics, the environment, sexuality, or the economy—the kinds of things people talk about when they do not think they are talking religion.[9]

Respect is crucial. One regrettable legacy of the pastoral counseling movement is its tendency toward psychological reductionism. As valuable as familiarity with basic psychological dynamics can be, and as much as we have learned from family systems theories applied to congregational life, such categories can be a snare for us. We can misuse them, overinterpreting the behavior of individuals and congregations, particularly when we do not like what's going on. So whenever we catch ourselves saying or thinking, "Oh, they're just working out their..." or "She simply never

---

9. Thomas C. Oden, *Pastoral Theology: Essentials of Ministry* (San Francisco: HarperCollins, 1983), 184.

came to terms with. . . , " a warning light should flash on. Even if our hunch has some truth in it, it is never the whole truth about someone. Because we are made in the image of God, each human being contains unfathomable depths.

French philosopher Simone Weil, whose writings on friendship are among the most probing in Christian thought, emphasized the positive role of distance in human relationships. By this she meant what the ascetical tradition has generally called "detachment": applied to human relationships, it refers to the interior freedom that allows us to respect the autonomy and liberty of another. In Weil's judgment, this quality of respectful distance in friendship also instructs us about human relationships in general. She understood true friendship to be a kind of "miracle," something that belongs to the "supernatural" order and depends upon grace. Moreover, she perceived a link between this kind of respectful, nonpossessive love and its source in the holy Trinity:

> Pure friendship is an image of that original and perfect friendship which belongs to the Trinity and which is the very essence of God. It is impossible for two human beings to be one while scrupulously respecting the distance which separates them, unless God is present in each of them.[10]

Something of the same respect, even reverence, comes into play in pastoral relationships, especially because people expose such tender parts of themselves to our scrutiny. They allow us to see them in their vulnerability, whether we are hearing confessions, visiting in the hospital, or sitting with a bereaved family. We know that we are invited into these places of pain and weakness simply because we are the priest; were it not for our ordination, we would not be there. The trust our parishioners bestow upon us confirms us in our vocation. We realize anew that people need a pastor— even more, they need God, the Good Shepherd, in whose name we minister, conveying his presence simply by our own.

---

10. Simone Weil, *Waiting for God,* trans. Emma Craufurd (London: Routledge and Kegan Paul, 1951), 136–37. See also the illuminating discussion of Weil's thought in Robert Davis Hughes III, *Beloved Dust: Tides of the Spirit in the Christian Life* (New York: Continuum, 2008), 280–96.

Even as our parishioners reach out to us, implicitly asking us to be Christ to them, we are permitted to see Christ in them—the Christ of a thousand faces. In the dying old man, unable to drink even a drop of liquid, his mouth and throat parched, we hear the unspoken words, "I thirst." In the anguished story of the woman abandoned by her husband, we catch sight of Christ deserted by his friends. In the parents at their wits' end over their son's drug addiction, we glimpse the father of the prodigal, helplessly waiting for his boy's return to sanity, health, and home. Pastor M. Craig Barnes writes of visiting a parishioner, an elderly man now living in a convalescent home. After a brief conversation, Barnes prayed what he called "the standard pastor-goes-to-the-nursing-home kind of prayer." But it triggered tears in Jack, his parishioner. Barnes waited in respectful silence. With just a bit of prompting, Jack explained, "You lose life in pieces. And then one day you find yourself here. . . . " That is how many of us die: first we lose this, then we lose that. Jack had lost his house, his dog, and the companionship of his wife, now in the Alzheimer's unit: "Jack's small, Spartan room makes it painfully clear that in the end we all die stripped of the things we spent a lifetime collecting."[11] The losses become progressively more costly, rapid, and closer to the bone. In the end we must surrender the last shred of life, the final breath: "Into your hands I commend my spirit."

It is during public liturgies of healing that the sense of divine presence to human suffering can be most palpable, especially when the emphasis is on prayer for the healing of body, mind, and spirit rather than a particular cure. The power of the service lies in its straightforward intercessory prayer, combined with trust in sacramental grace conveyed through the ordinary ministrations of the church. Many parishes offer the rite of anointing not only to individuals who are bedridden, in the hospital, or about to undergo surgery, but also to the whole congregation at a regularly scheduled eucharist.

In parishes I have served, not everyone came forward on these occasions for the laying on of hands and anointing. Those who

---

11. M. Craig Barnes, "Holy Ground: A Pastoral Call," in *The Christian Century* 126:10 (May 19, 2009): 10–11.

stayed in the pews, however, still took part in the service by adding their silent prayers of intercession, while those asking for anointing formed a semicircle before the altar and remained there together until the rite was completed. Some knelt at the rail; others placed a supportive hand on the shoulder of those being anointed. While the rite does not require participants to indicate what sort of healing they seek, nearly everyone did. The liturgy itself seems to create a kind of sanctuary, a holy space that can safely contain personal pain. Specific requests for healing, made quietly to the priest, were still within earshot of others. In some cases, the biddings went beyond the usual petitions for deliverance from physical ills or chronic conditions such as arthritis. People also exposed more sensitive areas: for example, their struggles with depression, anxiety, unresolved grief, or memories of abuse. This willingness to state plainly in a public setting one's sense of weakness and one's hopes for healing had several consequences for parish life.

These reserved, middle-class Episcopalians were clearly moved by the heartfelt prayer offered on these occasions. Parishioners who had previously felt insignificant suddenly knew themselves loved, as others gathered around them in prayer. We saw each other anew as suffering members of the body of Christ. Even when people had not stated the particular grace of healing that they desired, just showing up for the laying on of hands meant they stood in need of relief, as everyone recognized. Parishioners who had previously regarded some other members as difficult or irritating now discovered wellsprings of sympathy for those they glimpsed for a moment in their vulnerability. There was more pain in the parish than anyone had guessed; bearing it together, as we upheld one another in prayer, made it more endurable. We sensed the Holy Spirit praying in us, and we felt the touch of Christ in the laying on of hands. There was healing in those liturgies beyond what we had anticipated as charity deepened and faith grew stronger.

When she was dying of cancer, Rachel Hosmer of the Order of St. Helena would say, "I am dying and being healed at the same time." Any healing is a participation in the grace of the resurrection. The new life we now share with Christ comes to us from the future he holds for us, momentarily flaming up; it appears as a sign of the great healing still to come. Most of the time, however, we experience the paschal mystery as entering into the death of Christ, although for Christians the death and resurrection of Jesus are inextricably joined. "I want to know Christ and the power of his resurrection," writes Paul, "and the sharing of his sufferings by becoming like him in his death, if somehow I may attain the resurrection from the dead" (Phil. 3:10–11). Union with Christ in his death is the way into resurrection, and sometimes we experience both simultaneously.

When we minister to people in distress of any kind, we are being drawn with them into the mystery of the cross. A new pastor told me of visiting the home of a young man in his twenties stricken with inoperable brain cancer. The family wanted her to pray for a miraculous cure. Although she did pray with them for healing, she found she could not pray for the desired miracle. Upon later reflection, she realized that she was experiencing something of the same helplessness before this inexplicable illness as the man himself. He could do nothing about this brain tumor, either. What they could do was stand together in the darkness of uncertainty before God. The pastor could pray with him and his family, lifting up the enigma of disease, along with their fears and fearful hopes, to the still greater mystery of God. We can walk the way of the cross with our parishioners, holding the whole gamut of their feelings within the embrace of God.

As pastors we often find ourselves standing at the foot of the cross, witnessing searing human pain. Most of the time, we can do little to relieve it, and sometimes, in fact, it would be a mistake to try to rescue people from it. Habitual sin and foolish choices bring damaging consequences, and people usually need to face the cost of their decisions by themselves. Or they may be experiencing through the friction of human relationships the price of growing into greater human maturity. We can offer support, encourage perseverance, perhaps shed light on more or less helpful strategies, but we cannot take away the pain. It needs to do its work and cannot be circumvented. In his own pastoral practice, Jesus never did for others what they could do for themselves. He repeatedly summoned people to responsibility. Even when their wishes might seem obvious, he typically required them to exercise some initiative: "Do you want to be made well?" was his question to the paralytic (John 5:6). He would not act until asked.

But if we cannot—and in some cases, should not—relieve pain, we can sometimes interpret it by helping people notice where grace may be secretly at work, founded on the assurance that "all things work together for good for those who love God" (Rom. 8:28). This is neither baseless optimism nor fatalism—the false belief that the terrible things that happen to us "just had to be," as if God were in the habit of trumping human liberty. Rather, it is faith that God is present to us in every circumstance; because of God's faithfulness toward us, we can align ourselves with divine grace no matter what may befall us.

For pastors who regularly meditate on Scripture, integrating its perspective with their own, this interpretive approach to pastoral care will come as second nature. It means, of course, that we will have spent years wrestling with the enigmas of the texts and the shadows of life. It is not a matter of applying pat biblical analogies to every contemporary situation, but a way of experiencing everything that happens as taking place in Christ. So as we listen to our parishioners' anguish over a problem or come to grips with our own, we do so prayerfully, with an openness to the leading of the Spirit. We are not grasping after an answer, but gently placing ourselves in a posture of receptivity. We may wait a long time before we see where grace may be at work, and sometimes it is never clear. Even if we offer an interpretation, it is best presented tentatively. Our finest spiritual hunches have to be tested, typically through conversation, within the community of faith.

W.H. Vanstone's *The Stature of Waiting* offers a classic example of this process. Vanstone, himself a parish priest and student of the New Testament, saw the handing over of Jesus by Judas in Gethsemane as a pivotal moment in the passion story: from that point on, Jesus is someone more acted upon than an actor in the story. In reflecting theologically on the passion, Vanstone observes how so many of us find ourselves, like Jesus, in the grip of powerful forces and circumstances we cannot control. Family breakdowns, economic setbacks, illness and aging, losing a job or retiring from a career can force us from our primarily active role to one in which we are acted upon by others, in which we wait. People often undergo this change feeling diminished or degraded by it. Yet Vanstone looks to the passivity of Jesus in the passion story as a key to how God operates; in Jesus' acceptance of his passion he perceives pure, undefended love.

Pastoral interpretations such as these can offer genuine comfort. Our suffering does not go away, but it is released from meaninglessness. Although Christians regularly hear that baptism forges a union with Christ in his death and resurrection, we usually need our pastors to point out how that death and resurrection show up in the particular circumstances of our lives. We need coaching to lay hold of the paradoxical grace to which Paul gives voice: "We are afflicted in every way, but not crushed; perplexed, but not driven to despair; persecuted, but not forsaken; struck down, but not destroyed; always carrying in the body the death of Jesus, so that the life of Jesus may also be made visible in our bodies" (2 Cor. 4:8–10). Only the resurrection of Jesus can make this juxtaposition of suffering and joy possible.

This eschatological perspective, so crucial to pastoral oversight, will also condition the way we pray for others. In the "high priestly prayer" of John's gospel, it is significant that Jesus does not request deliverance from suffering for either himself or his disciples. Our own intercession for those in our pastoral care will often begin, if we are honest, with a frank request for relief. But over time, if we persevere, we may find ourselves with another prayer being formed in us that is more like the pastoral prayer of Jesus. Our desires will have sorted themselves out, with the most fundamental intentions coming to the fore. The bottomline for Jesus is not escape from pain, but freedom from sin: "I am not asking you to take them out of the world, but I ask you to protect them from the evil one" (John 17:15). To be taken "out of the world" would mean removal from the arena of struggle, hardship, and death. In the context of the high priestly prayer, this is the very entrance into glory, as Jesus is lifted up on the cross. What we want, for ourselves and others, is to be with him wherever he is.

In telling the story of his visit to the nursing home, significantly titled "Holy Ground," Craig Barnes begins by admitting that he had to be prompted to make this call by a church elder. Nobody wants to go to the convalescent home: not pastors, not the adult children of the residents, and certainly not the residents themselves. Who does not leave without thinking, once again, "I hope I don't end up in a place like that"? Our resistance to visiting the convalescent home is of a piece with the residents' own misery about being there. It smells of death, not life. Yet as he emerges from the facility, Barnes regains his balance in the crisp winter air: "I leaned against the hood of my car, looked up at the exterior window to Jack's room, and wondered if perhaps I had just been granted another visit to the Holy of Holies." Situated at the very center of the Jerusalem temple, the "holy of holies" was totally dark, stripped of all furnishings but an altar of sacrifice: "Jack did what every member of the priesthood of believers eventually has to do. In the end, we all place life on the altar before God. Sometimes all at once. More typically in pieces."[12]

Barnes calls himself a mere "witness" to Jack's sacrifice and wonders what prayer he could possibly have offered that would have been adequate. His misgivings serve as a warning against religious glibness. We do not want to sound like Job's comforters, offering rationalizations to soothe ourselves as much as the sufferer. Sometimes silence is the only response that might convey our reverence before the mystery of suffering, respecting pain that is not ours to endure. Yet I believe our witness also becomes, in some small measure, participation—sharing in the grace of the cross on the altar of sacrifice. We believe that Christ is fully present to his people in their afflictions, whether they happen to know it or not. Sometimes, like Barnes, we become aware of having brushed up against the holy in our pastoral work. Our witness, spoken simply and directly, testifies to the grace of God enfolded in these events.

So every pastoral encounter entails a degree of vulnerability for us. We spend a lot of time anticipating meetings of all sorts. We drive to the hospital after getting the call from Intensive Care. We wait for the couple to arrive for premarital counseling. We pre-

---

12. Barnes, "Holy Ground," 11.

pare to visit the family that is new to the congregation. We arrange the church or our office before hearing a confession to ensure uninterrupted privacy and quiet. We do not know for certain what any of these encounters will bring, but beneath them all is the invitation to be with God. We can approach these meetings with a contemplative receptivity, wondering how grace will open up in the course of conversation. The same holy expectancy can inform our work with committees and groups, including those whose outcomes we may dread. When we feel particularly vulnerable or anxious about any prospective encounter, it is worth pondering whether those with whom we will be engaged might be feeling the same way. Is there some underlying connective tissue that binds us to one another and to Christ?

Revisiting Holy Ground

"Feed my lambs. . . . Tend my sheep." (John 21:15–16)

Recent years have seen a movement away from a therapeutic, caregiving model of the pastoral vocation toward a more robust vision of pastoral oversight. Part of the problem with the therapeutic model for pastors was the uncritical adoption of values somewhat incongruous with Christian ministry. Some of the jargon is still around, such as the idea of a "nonjudgmental" approach to pastoral relationships. But all discernment entails some form of judgment: of right from wrong, of the good from the better, of the leading of the Holy Spirit, of the trickery of the Evil One. Pastors, in particular, are asked to interpret diverse situations in the light of the gospel. The net result of decades of "nonjudgmental" pastoring has been widespread ignorance of the Christian kerygma, incomprehension of basic theological doctrine, and moral drift. Confusion about the meaning of our vocation also leads to clerical exhaustion. As William Willimon notes:

Practicing what I have called "promiscuous ministry"—ministry with no internal, critical judgment about what is worth giving—we become victims of a culture of insatiable need. . . . In this vast supermarket of desire, we pastors must do more than simply "meet people's needs." The church is also about giving people the critical means of assessing which needs give our lives meaning, about giving us needs that we would not have if we had not met Jesus.[13]

The goal of pastoral ministry is directing people toward God. We hope to further the lifelong process of conversion: it is the aim of every sermon, every class, and every pastoral conversation. We may offer pastoral care, but we are not fundamentally "caregivers"; we may meet some legitimate needs, but our office is not that of a "needs-provider." We seek through our pastoral vocation the transformation of self and society that is marked by true holiness: "The fruit of the Spirit is love, joy, peace, patience, kindness, generosity, faithfulness, gentleness, and self-control" (Gal. 5:22–23). We yearn for the kingdom when God will be all in all, and we know that in Christ the glory is complete. Yet there will be resistance. Willimon, like Eugene Peterson, asks pastors to be realistic: our churches are made up of sinners. We should not be shocked when sin shows up, as it inevitably will. We must not pretend it is not there, but take it into account. Since we are sinners ourselves, we know how intractable and devious sin can be. Reflecting on the fact of sin in our congregations can put a lot of things in perspective; and it can, paradoxically enough, make us more humble and patient, as well as more resilient.

In the epilogue to John's gospel, Jesus hands over pastoral authority to Peter. Context is everything in this story. The charge to "feed my lambs, tend my sheep, feed my sheep" comes in the course of Peter's rehabilitation as a disciple. The charcoal fire and the threefold question of "Do you love me?" recall the scene of Peter's denial, now replayed. He gets to do it over, and this time he gets it right. Still, the interview with Jesus is poignant and hum-

---

13. William H. Willimon, *Pastor: The Theology and Practice of Ordained Ministry* (Nashville: Abingdon Press, 2002), 60.

bling for him: "Lord, you know everything; you know that I love you." He cannot get by with a general absolution. Peter must declare his love directly to Christ and publicly, too, before the other disciples.

As in the case of preaching, there is no pastoral charge unless we know we have been forgiven, because oversight demands a kind of preaching through our life and leadership; at every turn it should be pointing toward Christ. There is no pastoral office responsibly discharged unless it springs from our love for the Lord: "Yes, Lord; you know that I love you." We minister to others out of the depths of our own deliverance, salvation, and new life in Christ. Even when we say nothing in the face of inexplicable anguish, as sometimes we must, pastoral silence is full of faith, hope, and love. We can bear to be with others in excruciating pain because we are revisiting holy ground. Our confidence in divine love has been forged in the flames of our own suffering and guilt, transformed by the mercy of Christ.

CHAPTER FIVE

DEFYING AND
DEFINING LIMITS

Temptation in Ministry

*"And do not bring us to the time of trial, but rescue us
from the evil one." (Matthew 6:13)*

SO FAR WE HAVE been considering, for the most part, ways
in which we might experience the nearness of God in the ordinary practice of ministry. Grace confronts on all sides in a world
saturated with the presence of the Risen Christ (Eph. 4:10). Each
occasion brings the opportunity of a fresh encounter with our
Lord, discovering anew his abiding life among us. Yet we would
be naïve to suppose that the Holy Spirit is the only spirit around,
that all the influences that press upon us are benign. The biblical
tradition speaks of other forces at work in the world: some cosmic,
named as "principalities and powers"; and others more personal,
located in the figure of the tempter or Satan. The synoptic gospels
make a close connection between ministry and temptation, for all
three situate an experience of personal temptation immediately
before the beginning of Jesus' public life. These temptations attack
the core identity of Jesus, an identity that had just been revealed
at his baptism, and they seek to distort the character of his future

115

ministry. Temptation thus seems to be intertwined with both identity and ministry. Because the tempter wants to undo Jesus' ministry, he goes about it by attempting to subvert, ever so subtly, his
distinct identity—an identity grounded in his relationship to God.

Our own ministries are undermined in much the same way.
Evidences of evil bombards us: the casualties of war on the evening
news, the cheapening of human life in advertising and entertain-
ment, or the social inequalities in our own neighborhoods. Of
course, evil can also undermine itself by reminding us that we
stand in need of a savior, that we have, as one Lenten collect puts
it, "no power in ourselves to help ourselves" (BCP 218). The re-
nunciations of the baptismal rite give voice to our desire, at least
at the level of conscious intention, to set aside evil in its various
guises: the cosmic evil that we sense is larger than we are; the
twisted social forces that pervade and corrupt whole cultures; and
the undertow of evil at work within each of us.

Some people find any notion of a personal power of evil—
whom the gospels identify as Satan, the devil, or simply the Evil
One—obsolete, perhaps even laughable. But failure to recognize
the forces of evil at work in the world is a serious mistake.
Whether we understand the first baptismal renunciation—of
"Satan and all the spiritual forces of wickedness that rebel against
God"—as the repudiation of an intelligence operating independ-
ently of human beings or simply as a rejection of the evil residing
in the human psyche itself, the result, as Kenneth Leech has sagely
observed, is the same: "a reduction of human freedom, and spiritual disturbance." As Leech explains, "What is important in the
tradition of 'false spirits' is not the precise structure of de-
monology, but rather the existence of false spiritual directions,
false paths, idols which can become the focus of attention and di-
vert the soul toward a destructive and death-inducing spirituality."[1] One benefit of the traditional mythology is the way it locates
the origin of evil *outside* the human sphere. While we detect the
influence of evil within ourselves, in the ancient scheme evil is not
part of human nature as such; the Evil One is rather "the Enemy
of our human nature," as Ignatius of Loyola dubbed him. Evil

---

1. Kenneth Leech, *Soul Friend: The Practice of Christian Spirituality* (San Francisco:
Harper and Row, 1977), 131.

weakens and corrupts human beings, but it remains fundamentally alien to our true selves, especially as we recover our identity in Christ. Our susceptibility to temptation remains, but it does not define us.

While most people can acknowledge the fact of evil in human history, particularly in its more horrific manifestations, we are usually less sensitive to its subtler expressions. Temptation nonetheless assaults even the holiest of people, perhaps especially such people, since they are capable of accomplishing great good. Who better to undermine? People who are spiritually mature will not usually be drawn to monstrous sin (such temptations would be too obvious), but rather to small infidelities and slight compromises sufficient to undercut grace. As St. Paul observed of his own proclivities, "I find it to be a law that when I want to do what is good, evil lies close at hand" (Rom. 7:21). If we are going to speak of grace in ministry we must also speak of temptation in ministry.

The temptations of Christ get played out, in one way or another, in the interior struggles of all Christians. For us, as for Jesus, it is baptism that sets us up for this kind of spiritual testing. Temptation is surely an equal opportunity employer, but clergy are tried in ways peculiar to their distinct vocation in the church, just as other Christians are tempted in ways characteristic of their own callings. In discussing how the temptations of Christ figure in the life of the clergy, I will focus on Matthew's second, and Luke's third, temptation: the devil's suggestion that Jesus hurl himself from the pinnacle of the temple in Jerusalem. The presumption of immunity from foolish risk-taking is a common piece of clerical self-deception. For what appear to be the best of reasons, clergy seem prone to press beyond the bounds of what is humanly possible. I wish to concentrate on two distinct but related areas where failure to honor human limits is particularly apt to work havoc: in our relationships and in incessant overwork. To be sure, other failings exist in clergy, but I wish to focus on these two blind spots because, beyond the familiar rhetoric of "boundaries" and "self-care," the discipline and grace of embracing limitation has not been sufficiently explored; at least, it has yet to convince many of us to change longstanding patterns of behavior.

TEMPTED BY THE GOOD

"He was in the wilderness forty days, tempted by Satan." (Mark 1:13)

A good place to start is with an examination of the temptations of Jesus. Since it is his ministry in which we are engaged, we can safely assume that his temptations will also figure somehow in our own exercise of ministry. In fact, the story of the temptations of Christ throws a penetrating light on our own susceptibility to certain kinds of sin. The episode is situated prominently in the synoptic gospels, with Matthew and Luke, following Mark, placing them immediately after Jesus' baptism. Indeed, they are presented as something of a *consequence* of Jesus' baptism, and they form a connective link between the baptism and the public ministry of Jesus. Mark simply but forcefully asserts that "the Spirit immediately drove him out into the wilderness. He was in the wilderness forty days, tempted by Satan" (Mark 1:12–13). Matthew and Luke, however, offer a richly parabolic rendering of the temptations themselves.

The temptations of Christ are as problematic as they are fascinating. The very fact that Jesus could be tempted at all is an astonishing witness to his humanity. We experience temptation as a form of suffering, involving as it does a psychological state of interior division, of feeling pulled in two directions at once. Diogenes Allen, following Thomistic thought, maintains that we are rarely attracted by outright evil, only by lesser goods or by evils disguised as good: "We are not tempted into evil by things that are evil, but by things that are good or needful. The opening into the spiritual realm is blocked not by evil things, but by good ones. That is why renunciation is required of us—to give up something of value, to give up pearls for the one pearl of great price."[2]

To take the temptations of Christ seriously as genuine temptation—not as pretending or play-acting—is to take seriously the

2. Diogenes Allen, *Temptation* (New York: Church Publishing, 1986, 2004), 7–8.

Incarnation. It is strange to consider Jesus as open to possible deception, attracted even briefly to evil in disguise, cognizant of personal weakness, and vulnerable to spiritual assault. But all those limitations are involved in the experience of temptation. It is a situation as baffling to contemplate as Jesus' seeking out a baptism for repentance of sins. Yet his temptations are intimately tied to his baptism.

The baptism of Jesus is the first public event of his adult life described in the synoptic gospels. It is a perplexing event, and evidence within the gospel accounts indicates that it was troubling for the evangelists themselves, suggesting as it does an attitude of penitence and a felt need for spiritual cleansing on the part of Jesus—in sharp contrast to the emphatic assertion that Jesus was "without sin" in other parts of the New Testament tradition. The action is set in motion when Jesus deliberately offers himself as a candidate for John's baptism of repentance, thereby aligning himself with penitent sinners. Emerging from the Jordan, he is immediately proclaimed God's beloved Son, in language echoing the call of the Suffering Servant in Isaiah. For Jesus, as for us, baptism is a defining moment. He is anointed by the descending Spirit; and a voice from heaven names who he is—the beloved Son—just as he is about to embark on his mission.

Both parts of Jesus' baptismal experience must be held together: his insistence upon lowering himself into the waters of the Jordan with penitent sinners, on the one hand, and his vindication by God as his beloved Son, on the other. Indeed, the blessing of the divine Son seems to follow upon Jesus' humble association with sinners. God seems to be saying, "Yes! This is how my Son acts." As Martin Smith writes of this gospel moment: "God's pleasure in Jesus can no longer be contained, and it bursts out.... In the muddy river Jesus was taking on the role of representing Humanity, of being its suffering Heart and Self before God. As soon as Jesus had done that decisively, God flooded him with awareness of his unique relationship as Son and anointed him with the life-giving Breath for his mission."[3]

---

3. Martin L. Smith, *A Season for the Spirit* (Cambridge, Mass.: Cowley Publications, 1991), 9–10.

The vocation defined here, of being at once the "Son of God" and the "Son of Man"—that is, the representative of the human race in its weakness and sin—will spell degradation and suffering. This shame will carry forward to the cross, when Jesus is crucified between two criminals. The evangelists will turn to the Servant Songs to interpret this disgrace: in his passion narrative Luke (22:37) will recall Isaiah's "he was numbered with the transgressors" (53:12), a recollection that appears also in some manuscripts of Mark. From the beginning of his public life to its end outside the walls of Jerusalem, Jesus would refuse to "rise above" human weakness and dishonor, all the while holding fast to his relationship to God his Father.

It is precisely these two sides of sides of his identity—the divine son and the representative human—that are repeatedly assaulted by the tempter. The devil's opening gambit for two of the temptations, "If you are the Son of God," attacks the core of the relationship Jesus enjoys with his Father, the loving bond so recently revealed at his baptism. More subtly, however, each temptation in a different way also invites Jesus to throw off his kinship to the human race by transcending the limitations of his own humanity. For in the Jordan, as we have seen, Jesus chose to side with human beings as they actually are: sinful, weak, needy, and vulnerable.

Obviously, because of the highly symbolic portrayal of the temptations, they are open to a broad interpretation of meanings.[4] They are roomy enough for us to find our own infirmities lodged there. Notice particularly the scriptural verses Jesus selects to resist each demonic suggestion, powerful words that expose each temptation's fundamental deception, thus disarming the tempter, at least temporarily. Some aspects of the temptations, then, seem reasonably clear: By refusing to turn stones into bread, Jesus allows himself to suffer hunger rather than misuse spiritual power; there

---

4. Among modern interpretations see Dietrich Bonhoeffer, *Temptation,* ed. Eberhard Bethge and trans. Kathleen Downham (London: SCM Press, 1953, 1961); Henri J. M. Nouwen, "Temptation," in *Sojourners* 10 (July 1981): 25–27; Parker J. Palmer, "Jesus in the Desert," in *The Active Life* (San Francisco: Harper, 1990), 99–119; and Diogenes Allen, *Temptation.* In *Disordered Loves: Healing the Seven Deadly Sins* (Cambridge, Mass.: Cowley Publications, 1994), 26–29, William S. Stafford illuminates the tangled connections that exist among power, identity, and food in the first temptation of Christ.

exists a sharper hunger that neither bread, nor anything of this world, can fully satisfy. By refusing to invoke divine help to escape the consequences of self-imposed disasters, Jesus will not claim exemption from the constraints of ordinary creaturely life. And finally, by refusing to worship the Evil One, he will remain single minded in his devotion to God.

Thus all three temptations target Jesus' relation to his Father. The demonic taunt, "If you are the Son of God," together with the proposals that follow, seeks to redefine divine sonship. The tempter never articulates his own position, but works from unstated premises: of course, the Son of God should not suffer from hunger, the laws of gravity, or powerlessness. Better to undermine the bond between Jesus and his Father by insinuation than by outright frontal attack. What is at stake here is what it means to be the "Son of God." Underlying all the temptations is the attempt to subvert the relationship implied in the very word "Son." The beloved Son is called to fulfill the vocation of Israel's Suffering Servant, so rather than draw upon superhuman means to sidestep ordinary human frailty, the divine Son must embrace it.

In opposing the tempter, Jesus, characteristically, does not draw attention to himself. Rather, his counterattack is drawn directly from Scripture: "One does not live by bread alone, but by every word that comes from the mouth of God"; "Do not put the Lord your God to the test"; and "Worship the Lord your God, and serve only him" (Matt. 4:4, 7, 10). These verses from Deuteronomy accomplish the victory of Jesus in his desert testing, thus undoing the legacy of failure and disobedience to God recounted in the desert tradition of Israel. The story of Israel in the desert is recapitulated, and thus redeemed, in the obedience of Jesus in the desert.[5] Jesus' resistance to temptation sets him in right relationship to God.

---

5. The notion that Jesus' obedience "recapitulates" human history and thus redeems it figures prominently in the thought of St. Irenaeus. In his *Against the Heretics* (V. 21.2), he discusses the temptations of Jesus in the desert as an instance of this principle. However, Irenaeus, along with most other patristic commentators, understood the victory of Jesus in the desert as a reversal of the sin of Adam. Jesus undoes the disobedience of the Garden of Paradise by resisting, as our first parents did not, a temptation by way of food. See *Ancient Christian Commentary on Scripture*, vol. Ia, ed. Manlio Simonetti (Downers Grove, Ill.: InterVarsity Press, 2001), 56.

The story of the temptations also establishes Jesus in right relationship to us and to his own humanity. For in each case disobedience to God is cloaked in terms of false transcendence. The need for bread, for food, is real enough, but the tempter would have Jesus address his ordinary physical needs by using supernatural power, thus undercutting his baptismal commitment to ordinary humanity. Turning stones into bread would satisfy a legitimate human need by wrongly employing spiritual power and undo the very humility so pleasing to the Father. And as Jesus reminds the tempter, human beings have hungers that can only be satisfied by the word of God. However great his physical need, he will not quell his still greater craving for God in order to relieve it.

In the second and third temptations, the devil brings Jesus to a dizzying height: to the "pinnacle of the temple" and then to "a very high mountain." In both cases the very site of the temptations evokes a sense of being "above it all." In his final appeal, the devil offers Jesus the "glory" (*doxa*) of the kingdoms of the world; in Luke, the tempter throws in their "authority" (*exousia*) as well. Although these proposals smack of a crass bid for power, the seduction of prestige and influence in fact operates rather more subtly, particularly in the case of professedly religious people. As Henri Nouwen observes, "We make ourselves believe that striving for power and wanting to be of service are, for all practical purposes, the same. This fallacy is so deeply ingrained in our whole way of living that we do not hesitate to strive for influential positions in the conviction that we do so for the kingdom of God."[6]

The pursuit of power, even when rationalized as an opportunity for service, quickly becomes idolatrous. Hence Jesus' insistence: "Worship the Lord your God, and serve only him." And just as our relation to God becomes distorted in the quest for power, so does our relation to people. The ones we set out to serve eventually become a means to our ends—noble ends, we've convinced ourselves, but ends nonetheless. So for clergy, the congregation in the pews can cease to be the flock of Christ committed to their charge and instead turn into a set of encouraging statistics testifying to a "growing church." The adulation of power inverts

6. Nouwen, "Temptation," 27.

gospel values: those who work in poor rural communities or amid urban blight are perceived as those who could not land better positions; nonstipendiary ministry is disdained as the last option for clerical losers or misfits. Another casualty of "power ministries" are the small, hidden acts of service that loom large in God's eyes: visiting a convalescent home resident, preparing a simple meal well, sharing the pain of the bereaved, listening to a child talk about her day at school, taking out the trash, giving a cup of cold water in Christ's name. If what really counts is walking in the corridors of power, however local those corridors may be, we simply will not bother with the small stuff. We will not even notice that it is there.

The second temptation, that Jesus throw himself from the pinnacle of the temple, is the most elusive:

> Then the devil took him to the holy city and placed him on the pinnacle of the temple, saying to him, "If you are the Son of God, throw yourself down; for it is written, 'He will command his angels concerning you,' and 'On their hands they will bear you up, so that you will not dash your foot against a stone.'" Jesus said to him, "Again it is written, 'Do not put the Lord your God to the test.'" (Matt. 4:5–7)

Because the tempter's suggestion is so bizarre, so clearly symbolic, it is susceptible to a wide range of interpretations. Yet underlying all the temptations, including this one, is a common theme: that Jesus exploit his privileged relationship to God to rise above limitation. Each temptation develops this motif differently, yet in the second temptation it seems most pronounced because of the extravagance of the solution. People do find ways to satisfy their hunger and fulfill their needs for power, but not even a Houdini has managed a stunt like the one the tempter proposes when he takes Jesus to the pinnacle of the temple. Yet I believe this huge presumption points us to a rather commonplace sin.

"Do not put the Lord your God to the test": that is how Jesus frames the terms of this temptation. The tempter would have Jesus presume on God's loving care to save him from the recklessness of his own action. Here God would be invited, not to spare his righteous servant from unjust suffering (an issue dealt with variously in other parts of Scripture), but to save him from self-inflicted disaster. Jesus is supposed to move past the confines of creaturely existence and transcend the laws of nature, including those of his own human nature. He should press the boundary of the possible and reach beyond it. And God is invoked as a party to this plan.

ORDERING OUR SEXUAL SELVES

"Do you not know that your bodies are members of Christ?"
(1 Corinthians 6:15).

The unwillingness to live within our natural limitation that is so dramatically portrayed in the temptation narratives is everywhere apparent in our culture, and our propensity to overreach ourselves naturally affects all of our personal and social relationships because it is part of the cultural air we breathe. Nowhere is this more apparent than in marriage, where we must be willing to "forsake all others" in order to explore living with one spouse. We give up all other possible loves—past, present, and future—because experience, if nothing else, tells us that if we want depth we have to sacrifice breadth. However, marriage does not unfold in isolation, unless an *egoïsme à deux* has fatally warped the couple's relationship to society. Marriage contributes to and draws from a larger social fabric; for Christians, the marital relationship is situated, both theologically and experientially, in the church. Here again, married and covenanted Christians can be best sustained by the sacraments and fellowship of the church, while contributing to its strength of witness, if there is some degree of real continuity, over time, between these overlapping communities. Living within these practical limitations, both outside of and within marriage, is part of what the church has meant by the virtue of chastity.

When St. Paul upbraids the Corinthians for their lax attitudes toward sexual immorality, it is worth tracking his theological argument. Contrary to popular stereotype, his counsel is not based on disdain for the body or its sexual expression. Just the opposite. For Paul, everything comes back to one overwhelming reality: the resurrection. The resurrection of Jesus—the resurrection of his *body*—sanctifies our own bodies. The truth about our bodies, including our sexuality, can only be apprehended in the light of the resurrection: "Do you not know that your bodies are members of Christ?" (1 Cor. 6:15). Our baptismal union with Christ was costly in the extreme, but it opens a path for sanctification that embraces every aspect of our humanity, including the physical: "You were bought with a price; therefore glorify God in your body" (1 Cor. 6:20). Glorifying God in the body hints at a proleptic participation, even now, in the resurrection of the body. Our physical selves are holy.

And so when considering the meaning of sexual relationships, Paul, like Jesus, recalls the prelapsarian bliss of Eden. He returns to the creation story to describe the effect of sexual intercourse: "The two shall become one flesh" (Gen. 2:24; Matt. 19:5; 1 Cor. 6:16). Sexual immorality, by contrast, generates a sense of alienation from one's partner and from oneself. When sexual encounters are superficial and transitory, we cannot fully identify with our own sexual acts, for they fail to convey continuity with the self. Yet Paul maintains that something greater than the two sexual partners is at work even here, making them "one flesh." How many times can the self be parceled out and still maintain any sense of integrity, of wholeness? The Genesis tradition echoed in these New Testament texts, by contrast, proclaims a sexual union that constitutes a full expression of one's deepest self. Intercourse is truly creative: perhaps of a child, but more fundamentally of a relationship. It creates something new: one flesh, a genuine coupling, a freshly minted identity of unity-in-plurality, yet with each person remaining distinct. Helen Oppenheimer reflects on the profundity of this biblical vision and its congruence with real, not fancifully romantic, human experience, when she writes: "From the doctrine of the Trinity in heaven to the marriage bond on earth one can recognize built into the structure of reality, forms of union which do not swallow up or confound the persons entering into them but even enhance their distinctiveness."[7]

Yet many Christians remain captured by the romantic myths circulating in our culture, the outgrowth of the courtly love tradition that developed in the high Middle Ages.[8] Anyone engaged in regular premarital counseling will only rarely find couples who are free of it. For instance, the belief that "true love," especially when enshrined in matrimony, will somehow protect one from falling in love with someone other than one's spouse is widely, if unreflectively, held. If only love were so easy! It usually takes a bit of work to help couples realize that their hormones know nothing about marriage vows, and that human beings are so affectively constituted that we can easily fall in love with many potential candidates. The marriage vows are therefore constitutive of marriage: the public promise to take *this* person, and no other, for life, in a sexually exclusive union. It entails a profound acceptance of limitation. And as Thomas Breidenthal has pointed out, the vows are made unilaterally: that is why the hands are joined, then loosed, and then joined again as each set of vows is made. To be sure, no marriage would exist if both partners did not make these vows; but neither party makes the vows conditionally upon the other's.[9]

Christian marriage creates a "school of charity" in which one slowly learns how to love. Contemporary western marriage nearly always begins, at least at the courtship stage, with the delightfully effervescent experience of being "in love." But if the initial, exuberant sensation of being in love is for us an essential ingredient of marriage, it must nevertheless undergo a lifetime of purification. Eventually, romantic love must give way to mature love: the path of availability, respect, humility, generosity, forgiveness, and kindness described by Paul in 1 Corinthians 13. Jesus said that

---

7. Helen Oppenheimer, "Two Shall Become One" in *Men and Women: Sexual Ethics in Turbulent Times,* ed. Philip Turner (Cambridge, Mass.: Cowley Publications, 1989), 106.

8. See Rodney Clapp, "From Family Values to Family Virtues," in *Virtues and Practices in the Christian Tradition: Christian Ethics after MacIntyre,* ed. Nancy Murphy, Brad J. Kallenberg, and Mark Theissen Nation (Harrisburg, Pa.: Trinity Press International, 1997), 185–211, for a thoughtful, if somewhat severe, treatment of this phenomenon.

9. Thomas E. Breidenthal, *Christian Households: The Sanctification of Nearness* (Cambridge, Mass.: Cowley Publications, 1997), 90.

the greatest love entailed laying down one's life for one's friends (John 15:13), and for most people the commitment of marriage or of lifelong partnership serves as a suitable context to become schooled in its practice. As Robert Hughes astutely notes, "for married Christians marriage is the principal means of daily formation."[10]

Unfortunately for many people, including some clergy, the sway of romantic notions of love is so powerful that when they find themselves "falling out of love" with their spouses they panic, concluding that they must have somehow made a terrible error by getting married in the first place. Sometimes the tenets of neo-Romanticism are so uncritically accepted that people actually imagine they are morally obliged to dissolve the marriage if they no longer "love" their spouse. The possible causes of genuine marital failure are numerous and usually convoluted; but they can never be attributed to the mere cessation of heightened emotional engagement—unless, of course, in an attempt to keep ourselves on a perpetual emotional high, we violate the marriage by having an affair. Certainly taking the vows of marriage obliges us, at the very least, to seek both pastoral and professional help when our marriages are in jeopardy, engaging in this hard work with the intention of growing into a more realistic, reconstituted relationship. Our faith and hope for our marriages are not, finally, grounded in ourselves, but in the faithfulness of God, whose grace joined us together. When we feel our relationships are collapsing, the Holy Spirit may be drawing us into a new level of maturity in Christ, as we relinquish expectations that are simply not viable. Such growth will not be easy: the paschal mystery of Christ's death and resurrection is stamped on every aspect of Christian life. If we were bought with a price, our salvation will cost us something, too.

The sexual lapses of clergy have been a favorite subject for novels and films for decades, while parodies of the lecherous priest in art and drama stretch back at least to the Middle Ages. Perhaps be-

---

10. Robert Davis Hughes III, *Beloved Dust: Tides of the Spirit in the Christian Life* (New York: Continuum, 2008), 347. See especially his chapter on "Love of Friendship and Life in Community" for a probing discussion of this topic, including the formative graces of parenting for the parents. See also Breidenthal, *Christian Households.*

cause chastity is a hard-won virtue for most people, whether married or single, the sins of the clergy in this regard are especially targeted for ridicule. We are not only supposed to represent a higher standard of sexual probity; we are also perceived as the perpetrators of this difficult discipline. Be that as it may, people are rightly dismayed and scandalized when clergy abuse their positions of trust to seduce members of their parishes or, worst of all, victimize children. The justifiable outrage at such clerical betrayals, not to mention the pressure exerted by insurance companies, has led to the widespread education and reeducation of clergy and laity about creating safe environments in our churches.

Yet confusion about Christian sexual mores is still prevalent, and the undoing of priestly vocations, with the concomitant breakdown of clerical families, is still common. The recent popularity of the Starbridge novels of Susan Howatch among seminarians and clergy was due to more than their theological sophistication. For many people, these stories of talented and highly placed clergymen in the Church of England, rendered in a series of novels set over the course of the twentieth century, accurately depicted the manifold strains and temptations faced by many priests and their families. The clerical affairs that pepper these works of fiction do not portray monsters preying upon parishioners or children, but rather men caught in more commonplace adultery and fornication. The unraveling of their lives is instructive. Those in positions of power seem more susceptible to adultery: Are such men used to getting their own way? Do they believe themselves exempt from the ordinary constraints binding on the rest of mortals? Sometimes priests, like other people, seek illicit sex for sheer physical relief; more typically, they venture into other beds out of loneliness and desperate bids for affection. In many cases, they are themselves victims of a romantic ideology, taken by surprise by the depth of their own feelings for another, at a loss about how to negotiate passions they never dreamed they would have.

I doubt that clergy are greater sinners in sexual matters than the general population, but our public falls from grace are more scandalous and usually more damaging to our communities. Beyond our captivity to the romantic Zeitgeist of our age, however, there may be aspects of the typical clerical profile that perhaps set us up for trouble. For good and ill, we tend to be people who care considerably about the feelings of others. Indeed as a group we seem finely tuned emotionally, so finding appropriate outlets for our own affective expression will be crucial. We are also the bearers of many secrets. The spiritual intimacy of some pastoral conversations and situations can sometimes be burdensome; it can also create a craving for intensity in everyday relationships that tends to increase over time.

Both these possibilities point to the urgency of our finding ways to be honest: with God in prayer; with a spiritual director or confessor; and with close friends who are willing to be candid with us. We are all sinners; but in real life as in novels, clergy who fall most steeply into sin are almost always people who have isolated themselves spiritually. They may have many acquaintances and be highly popular and ecclesiastically successful, but they have no real pastor for themselves, someone whom they trust enough to risk personal transparency. This is a form of hubris: the prideful withdrawal from accountability to others, an unwillingness to concede to another Christian some measure of authority over our souls. We will not face the human limitation that we cannot be pastors for ourselves, no matter how smart we think we are, and so we "hurl ourselves down" as the tempter suggests, in confusion or defiance or both.

"Safe church training" has instilled in most of us an awareness of our responsibilities toward our parishioners with respect to sexual boundaries. Single clergy, for instance, may not date members of their congregations; and no one should transgress pastoral trust by any romantic overture or sexual liaison with those under their spiritual care. Even the appearance of scandal—by private meetings, for example—must be avoided whenever practical. Yet these guidelines, valuable as they are, leave unaddressed a host of situations that do not directly involve our parishioners: our relations to our friends and colleagues.

Many seminarians and clergy, for example, seem unprepared for the close bonds they may form with colleagues. Participation in diocesan committees and other, non-parochial groups provide additional occasions to form connections with lay and clerical members. We make friendships with both sexes, some of them lifelong, in seminary, naturally gravitating toward people who share our interests and our theological passions. Many of those with whom we enjoy professional or social ties are bright, sensitive, compassionate, and wise. We may find that we easily move to discussing our ideas, concerns, and aspirations. In time, we may disclose more personal issues and problems to these friends; we are, after all, trained to be good listeners. Before long, we are falling in love—and feeling guilty and bewildered to boot. How did something so good lead us down this path?

Friendship enriches and sustain our emotional and spiritual lives; for Christians, it offers training in the practice of godly love. Writing of the spiritual significance of our closest human relationships, Thomas Breidenthal observes that "marriage and life partnership, parenthood, friendship, and monastic community" all "invite us to learn with a limited number of people the demands and the joys of that nearness that will know no limits in the kingdom of God."[11] The relative emotional exclusivity of friendship, like the absolute sexual exclusivity of marriage, teaches us patterns of disciplined love. By accepting these relationships with all their limitations we are, paradoxically, being conditioned for the practice of an all-embracing charity. For this reason clergy should not be frightened away from friendship in an attempt to flee its possible pitfalls. There are, however, some crucial limits to be observed in our friendships, particularly those that might be liable to a romantic charge that could compromise our other commitments.

Since antiquity, philosophers have pondered the nature of true friendship. Drawing on this classical tradition, particularly Cicero's *On Friendship*, the twelfth-century Cistercian monk Aelred of Rievaulx composed his own treatise for his fellow monks, *On Spiritual Friendship*. It still repays reading. Aelred emphasizes an ingredient essential to all Christian friendship worthy of the name: a common commitment to virtue. Christian friends must be

11. Breidenthal, *Christian Households*, 40.

joined in their desire to please God, not just each other. What they will want above all for each other, as well as for themselves, is growth in the life of grace and true holiness. Without this core commitment, there exists mere camaraderie—a pleasant form of companionship, perhaps, but not a true Christian friendship.

When our friendships are enjoyed as part of our fellowship in Christ, therefore, we wish no harm—particularly no spiritual harm—to each other. When we engage in friendships with the potential for sexual attraction, some of the same precautions come into play that we observe in our relations to parishioners. We meet one another only in public places, for instance, and we do not keep the friendship secret, especially not from our spouse or partner. We guard our hearts, and observe modesty of behavior and conversation. If we find our affections aroused, or if we find ourselves making comparisons unflattering to our spouse, it is essential to make this known to our spiritual director and confessor and, if necessary, we will need to end the friendship.

Chastity invites us to foster the "single eye." It is a reflection of the pure fire of divine love for us. Yet we are pulled in many directions: the body may crave one thing, the emotions another, the spirit yet another. We were made for friendship with God and communion with one another in Christ. All aspects of our lives belong to God, are part of the fellowship of the church, and can witness to divine grace and mercy. Nothing is left out. Short of our participation in resurrection glory, however, we are bound to feel the tension of the divided self, at some times more than others. "Seek first the kingdom of God and his righteousness": that is the antidote to our fragmented selves. It means, of course, setting priorities, and admitting we can't have it all. Part of living into the cross is accepting its constriction, but the narrow way turns out to be a birth passage into life, after all. Trying to order rightly our sexual selves, including our imaginations as well as our behavior, is not prudish lovelessness—just the opposite. It is a matter of training in love, with God's utter faithfulness to us making our own attempts at love possible. As William Stafford notes, "God's perseverance in love is the standard for ours, and human perseverance in love teaches us about God's faithfulness. God keeps his vows."[12] The disparate pieces of our lives can begin to fall into place, as we discover ourselves at last aligned with grace.

SUSTAINING PRAYER

"There is need of only one thing." (Luke 10:42)

Overwork sets us up for temptation and is a temptation in itself. There is plenty of work to do in the church: we catch a glimpse of the Apostle Paul's pastoral cares when, after recounting his sufferings at the hands of unbelievers, he adds, almost as an afterthought, "besides other things, I am under daily pressure because of my anxiety for all the churches" (2 Cor. 11:28). The gospels tell us that Jesus was at times so engulfed by human need that neither he nor his disciples could spare the time to eat (Mark 3:20). Christian ministry, when faithfully performed, has never been a leisurely profession.[13]

Yet the gospels also make it clear that Jesus balanced periods of feverish activity with times of solitude and prayer. He would wake before dawn to pray by himself (Mark 1:35) and sometimes withdrew to the mountains for retreat from the crowds (Mark 6:46). He urged his disciples, upon their return from the intensity of a mission, to "Come away to a deserted place all by yourselves and rest a while" (Mark 6:31). Despite his willingness to heal on the sabbath, which angered the religious leadership, Jesus perceived sabbath rest as God's gift to us rather than as an obligation we discharge toward God: "The sabbath was made for humankind, and not humankind for the sabbath" (Mark 2:27). In the precious glimpses the gospels afford us of Jesus' day-to-day activities, we

---

12. Stafford, *Disordered Loves,* 42.
13. In *Pastor: The Theology and Practice of Ordained Ministry* (Nashville: Abingdon Press, 2002), 315–25, William H. Willimon recounts some of the peculiar burdens of ordained ministry. Some of his observations, such as "The work of the church is never done," also disclose conditions ripe for clerical temptation.

see a demanding ministry offset by periods of personal prayer, synagogue worship, and meals with friends and disciples.

In recognition of our ongoing need for regular periods of rest, for observing the "sabbath principle," and for establishing a measure of equilibrium in our frenzied schedules, clergy in recent years have been regularly exhorted to practice "self-care." Time-honored traditions such as a "rule of life" and a "rule of prayer" have been rediscovered as tools for maintaining balance and due proportion. We are reminded to honor our bodies as well as our souls; that regular exercise and healthful diet are aspects of the stewardship of our bodies. Our primary emotional relationships in our families and with our friends deserve time and nurture, while regular study is crucial to priestly ministry and spirituality, as are periods of silent retreat. Above all, prayer remains essential—the very heartbeat of Christian life.

Yet many of us do not hear these recommendations as good news at all. Repeated exhortations to "self-care" can seem like one more burden placed on an already crowded schedule. We are not only frustrated by our inability to find time for ourselves; we are made to feel guilty for our hard work. We may not even be sure we agree that a wholly balanced life ought to be our goal: there may be aspects of the rhetoric of "self-care" that make us uneasy. The standard of "health and wholeness," terms sometimes used as virtually synonymous with "salvation," may strike us as more nearly akin to the personal culture movement than to the gospel. What, we may wonder, happened to self-sacrifice as a Christian ideal? Didn't Paul claim, when finding himself on the brink of death, that his life had been "poured out as a libation" (Phil. 2:17)?

Although healing of both mind and body figure significantly in the ministry of Jesus and serve as signs of the kingdom of God, it is another matter altogether to regard physical or even complete psychological health as a necessary ingredient of Christian holiness. For many of us, the way of grace may entail something quite different: bearing physical illness, accepting a disability, or enduring the limitations of our psychological makeup. Kenneth Leech, Philip Sheldrake, and Rowan Williams have all redefined what "wholeness" might be for the Christian this side of the eschaton.

In many cases, the wholeness available to us may consist in acknowledging the damaged elements of our past as part of the totality of our personal constitution. It is full acceptance of our history, scars and all, that can free us to love others who are also wounded, as indeed all human beings are in one degree or another. As Archbishop Williams writes:

> Far from isolating me, my suffering creates an intense solidarity with the whole human world; I can recognize my condition as more than mine alone. I can become truly "catholic," responsive to the needs of all. My pain has given me a key to love. And what is more, that love can coexist even with the continuation of feelings of fear and self-doubt. There will be for many no resolution into painlessness, into a "health" in which scars and injuries will vanish. The wholeness of holiness is not that.[14]

According to Paul, we can meet God everywhere and in everything. All our activities should be consecrated to divine service: "Whether you eat or drink, or whatever you do, do everything for the glory of God" (1 Cor. 10:31). If actions performed for the glory of God are as valuable in God's eyes as periods given to personal prayer (and presumably they are), the question still remains: What makes it actually possible for us to approach our various duties as a form of praise? How indeed do we "find God in all things" or "practice the presence of God" without some time apart for reflection on the course of our lives and conscious engagement with God? Are we not expecting the angels to come to our rescue if we throw ourselves off the pinnacle of a brutal work schedule? When we refuse to honor the limitations of our human nature, do we expect that God will somehow preserve us from physical exhaustion and interior depletion?

---

14. "The Abbé Huvelin: A University Sermon for All Saints' Day," in *A Ray of Darkness* (Cambridge, Mass.: Cowley Publications, 1995), 181–82. See also Philip Sheldrake, *Images of Holiness: Explorations in Contemporary Spirituality* (London: Darton, Longman and Todd, 1987), 28–31. Kenneth Leech discusses the similarities and distinctions between spiritual direction and therapeutic counseling, including their notions of health and wholeness, in *Soul Friend* (San Francisco: Harper, 1977, 1980), 90–136; see also his *The Social God* (London: Sheldon Press, 1981), 72–80.

It is not humanly possible to turn our work into prayer without some protected times for communion with God. Conversion of mind, of our habitual ways of looking at things, is a slow process. It takes a long time for grace to transform our outlook so completely that we bring a steady mindfulness of God's presence to all our activities. Such a profound change cannot take place unless we deliberately open ourselves to the transforming work of the Spirit. The practice of waiting upon God in various forms of prayer and meditation requires vulnerability and a willingness to undergo conversion of heart again and again. Through such prayerful disciplines, as Sarah Coakley reminds us, we "cease to set the agenda" and "'make space' for God to be God."[15] Over the long haul such practice is transformative, mysteriously shaping the pattern of Christ's death and resurrection within us.

How priests might use what has come to be called "quiet time with God" is wide-ranging. Highly structured methods of meditation are not necessary, although helpful to some.[16] Some people can pray while walking or while engaged in rhythmic motions; others require physical stillness to attend to God. Some use repetitive prayers such as the Jesus prayer or the rosary with profit. Still others find it natural simply to converse with God, perhaps alternating such colloquy with silence or meditative reading. Some engage in prayer without words, silently directing their loving attention toward God, while others use the methods of centering prayer to create an open space for God.

In the past thirty years, the centering prayer movement has introduced a form of contemplative prayer that is based on the *via negativa* or apophatic tradition. It is a method of prayer that requires emptying the mind of particular thoughts. In the theological tradition of the church, the *via negativa* developed as a strain of spirituality based on the insight that God always exceeds anything that we can manage to say or think about him. God is the "ever greater." When used as a form of meditation, the negative way consists of systematically letting go of every thought we might

---

15. Sarah Coakley, *Powers and Submissions: Spirituality, Philosophy and Gender* (Malden, Mass.: Blackwell, 2002), 34–35.
16. Sheldrake, *Images of Holiness,* 80–81.

entertain about God (since all fall short of the ultimate, incomprehensible reality) until, coming to the end of our rope, we let go. Here mystical writers revert to paradox and metaphor to explain how this experience of emptiness is simultaneously one of fullness, or how this darkness seems charged with light. St. John of the Cross speaks of it as a "luminous darkness." *The Cloud of Unknowing* observes that when we sense utter nothingness, "Our inward man calls it All." This may seem like pretty heady stuff. But it is really no more obscure than the gospel sayings about losing your life to find it. We never get to the bottom of these paradoxes. Instead, we move into their truth at deeper and deeper levels.

By coming into contact with this aspect of the contemplative tradition through the centering prayer movement, numerous people, many for the first time, have come to realize that it is possible to pray without words and even without thoughts. They have experienced a depth of connection to the Spirit who, as Paul testifies, can pray in us "with sighs too deep for words." Many dedicated practitioners have embarked upon a disciplined program of two twenty-minute periods of silence for centering each day. For them, centering prayer has opened a way into the heart of the divine mystery and it has been transformative.

Centering prayer, however, is not for everyone. For one thing, there are more methods of apophatic spirituality than the one taught by centering prayer; and there are many people who are not constitutionally suited to go the negative way, for another. Nor do they need to. The monastic tradition of meditative prayer, from which centering prayer itself springs, suggests that the negative path is usually trod only after extensive training in the affirmative way, and even then it remains a distinct call. More typically, one meditates using words and thoughts and images. The most widely practiced form of Christian meditation over the centuries has been *lectio divina*—meditating on a sacred text, usually Scripture. Two of the greatest exponents of the *via negativa* in the western Christian tradition, the author of *The Cloud of Unknowing* and St. John of the Cross, both insist that extended engagement with ordinary, discursive meditation precede apophatic contemplation. You don't give up discursive meditation, according to John of the Cross, until it becomes impossible for you to do it. And far from being an inferior form of prayer, meditation based on words and images sustained some of the greatest mystics of the church, including Bernard of Clairvaux, Julian of Norwich, and Teresa of Avila.

In my own experience, the relationship between the negative and the affirmative ways is more fluid than some earlier spiritual writers would have us think. Apophatic prayer is not always something you "arrive" at after years of seasoning in the affirmative (or *kataphatic*) way and then go on to maintain for the rest of your life. It is more complex than the assumption of a straight "progression" from discursive meditation to silent contemplative prayer would suggest. The centering prayer movement in the church has shown that people with little or no previous meditative background can engage in contemplative prayer without thoughts and words. By the same token, people who have been introduced to the awesome reality of God through this method sometimes need to return to the more common path of *lectio divina*. The strenuous discipline of setting aside every thought is either more than they can sustain or they find that they need to be formed by a more grounded engagement with God through the scriptural word—or both. Still others move back and forth between these methods of meditation with great freedom, finding one or another approach more suitable to different seasons in life.

Affective spirituality—forms of personal prayer that stress the place of love—has taken innumerable forms over the centuries. Some have been incorporated into the *via negativa;* others, into the *via affirmativa,* which retains thoughts, words, and images as a way into God. When medieval Christians developed the *via negativa* into a method of prayer, the role of love came to the fore. Maybe our thinking about God would never be adequate to the task, but love could still reach out blindly toward God, even as God reached toward us. Yet affective spirituality also finds expression in less austere modes, ranging from the tender, domestic incarnationalism of Franciscan piety, delighting in the Christmas crèche, for instance, to forms of simplified contemplation. The proverbial tale of the peasant who sat before the Blessed Sacrament for long stretches each day—"I just look at him and he looks at me"—is really a form of affective contemplation. So is gazing upon an icon with devotion or simply sitting still in the presence of Christ. Finally, the practice of *lectio divina,* the slow, meditative reading of Scripture, represents the longest tradition of Christian meditative practice. What is important in all of these cases is not so much the method employed as clearing a space for real engagement with God.

In periods of solitary reflection we discover why the Spirit drives us, as the Spirit drove Jesus, into the wilderness: first of all, to confront our own demons in the form of disordered passions and desires, our inner noise and turmoil. What Thomas Merton says of the monastic solitary applies also to those who practice solitude only on occasion:

> The Christian solitary is left alone with God to fight out the question of who he really is. . . . Do you want to be yourself or don't you? Do you insist on fighting the images of other people? Must you live as a symbolic appendage to somebody else that you desire or hate? Are you going to stand on your own two feet before God and the world and take full responsibility for your own life?"[17]

Without the rigorous honesty that solitude can engender, our words and actions quickly become shallow; our motives are soon compromised; and our discernment of what we should be doing—never an easy task, in any case—becomes even more faulty. Merton sees the immediate application of the discipline of solitude to the practice of ministry:

> What is the relation of all this to action? Simply this. He who attempts to act and do things for others or for the world without deepening his own self-understanding, freedom, integrity, and capacity to love, will not have anything to give to others. He will communicate to them nothing but the contagion of his own obsessions, his aggressiveness,

17. Thomas Merton, *Contemplation in a World of Action* (Garden City, N.Y.: Doubleday, 1965, 1971), 244.

his ego-centered ambitions, his delusions about ends and means, his doctrinaire prejudices and ideas.[18]

Yet the wilderness of the interior desert is not simply a place of unrelieved spiritual struggle. If we are indeed led by the Spirit into the desert, the anguish involved in confronting the self eventually gives way to an encounter with divine truth and mercy: "Those who go through the desolate valley will find it a place of springs" (Psalm 84:5). If the saints teach that painfully acquired self-knowledge must precede any knowledge we might gain of God, it is only so our true self might encounter the true God—and so be transformed. The human spirit longs for God and, as St. Augustine famously observed, our hearts are restless until they rest in God.

Because human beings are created for eternal joy with God, those Christians whose circumstances deny them occasions for solitude and personal prayer will undergo real suffering and loss.[19] It is not a condition to be readily accepted. This is life compromised by the Evil One, "the enemy of our human nature." A life without enough leisure for prayer—or for that matter, for other dimensions of human existence, such as physical exercise or the cultivation of friendship—is an inhuman life. Only a false asceticism would claim that Christian self-sacrifice requires an unrelieved, exhausting round of work. Christ's self-emptying of his divine prerogatives, the *kenosis* of Philippians 2, does not invite us to become hollow shells of humanity, spiritually bankrupt and physically depleted. On the contrary, it suggests that Christ accomplished the work of salvation by fully accepting the constraints of human nature. Insofar as Paul exhorts the Christians at Philippi to imitate Christ, he urges them to practice mutual deference, not self-destruction, in order to maintain harmony within the community (Phil. 2:1–5). When Paul does speak of the Christian's participation in the cross of Christ, he is referring to a spiritual "death to sin" such as that implicit in baptism (Rom. 6:3–11). Other sufferings for the sake of the gospel, including martyrdom,

---

18. Merton, *Contemplation in a World of Action*, 164.
19. Sheldrake, *Images of Holiness*, 89.

may come our way; but there is no suggestion in the New Testament that we should seek them out.

In the community of faith we need one another's support and strength to persevere in habits that are decidedly countercultural. Given all the pressures clergy face, it is important to look for ways to streamline the work of the church itself in order to concentrate on the essentials. A great many clergy allow their time to be eaten away by trivia. The essential work of being "pastor, priest, and teacher" to our people—and the disciplines of prayer and study that undergird these ministries—then ends up being pushed to the side. What Merton observed decades ago about church institutions is still apt: "In all forms of communal life we tend to multiply *useless* activities—time-consuming obsessions which for psychological reasons we are unable to abandon."[20] Although spirituality has come to the fore in recent decades, and we pay lip service to the fact that mature discipleship requires a serious commitment to prayer, there seems to be little willingness to pare down our workload to make prayer and a human pace of life actually possible. If we are going to take something on, just what are we going to let go? We need to cultivate the habit of recognizing limitation in order to practice the right ordering of our homes, dioceses, parishes, schools, and workplaces. Are we afraid that others will accuse us of failing to pull our weight—the accusation Martha of Bethany makes against her sister? Yet like Mary, we do well to claim time with the Lord, to pursue the "one thing needful" (Luke 10:38–42).

Sometimes resistance to prayer comes from within ourselves. We may be so conditioned by our culture that we cannot think of ourselves except in terms of productivity: what counts in our world is getting things done. We may feel genuinely conflicted by the numerous expectations placed upon us. Yet we know that continuing at our present pace, ignoring our yearning for God, is tempting fate, refusing to accept the limitations and requirements of our human nature. It is tantamount to throwing ourselves from the pinnacle of the temple.

---

20. Merton, *Contemplation in a World of Action*, 240.

But aside from the danger of burnout or the danger of falling into a sexual or other scandal, there is a deeper reason for attending to our soul's longing. No one is simply a worker; and we do not pray, read, or meditate simply to "refuel" in order to carry on with ministry. In John's gospel, the image of "servant" is balanced by that of "friend": "I do not call you servants any longer, because the servant does not know what the master is doing; but I have called you friends, because I have made known to you everything that I have heard from my Father" (John 15:15). The accent here falls on relationship rather than service. Service, of course, continues, but it is exercised within the framework of intimate, and mutual, self-disclosure. In prayer we open ourselves to God. Even more, by the impulse of the Spirit, we become the recipients of divine self-communication. Space for prayer, for delving into the mystery of this relationship with God, is not just another obligation we must add to the day's agenda. It is God's gift to us, and we are asked to make a place to receive it. No one, Paul assures us, is an expert in prayer, but our very ineptitude makes it possible for the Spirit to shape our prayer, inarticulate groanings "too deep for words." The Spirit who dwells in our hearts can then draw us into the prayer of Christ, and through Christ, into the very life of the Trinity.